Have I Got A
STORY
To Tell You

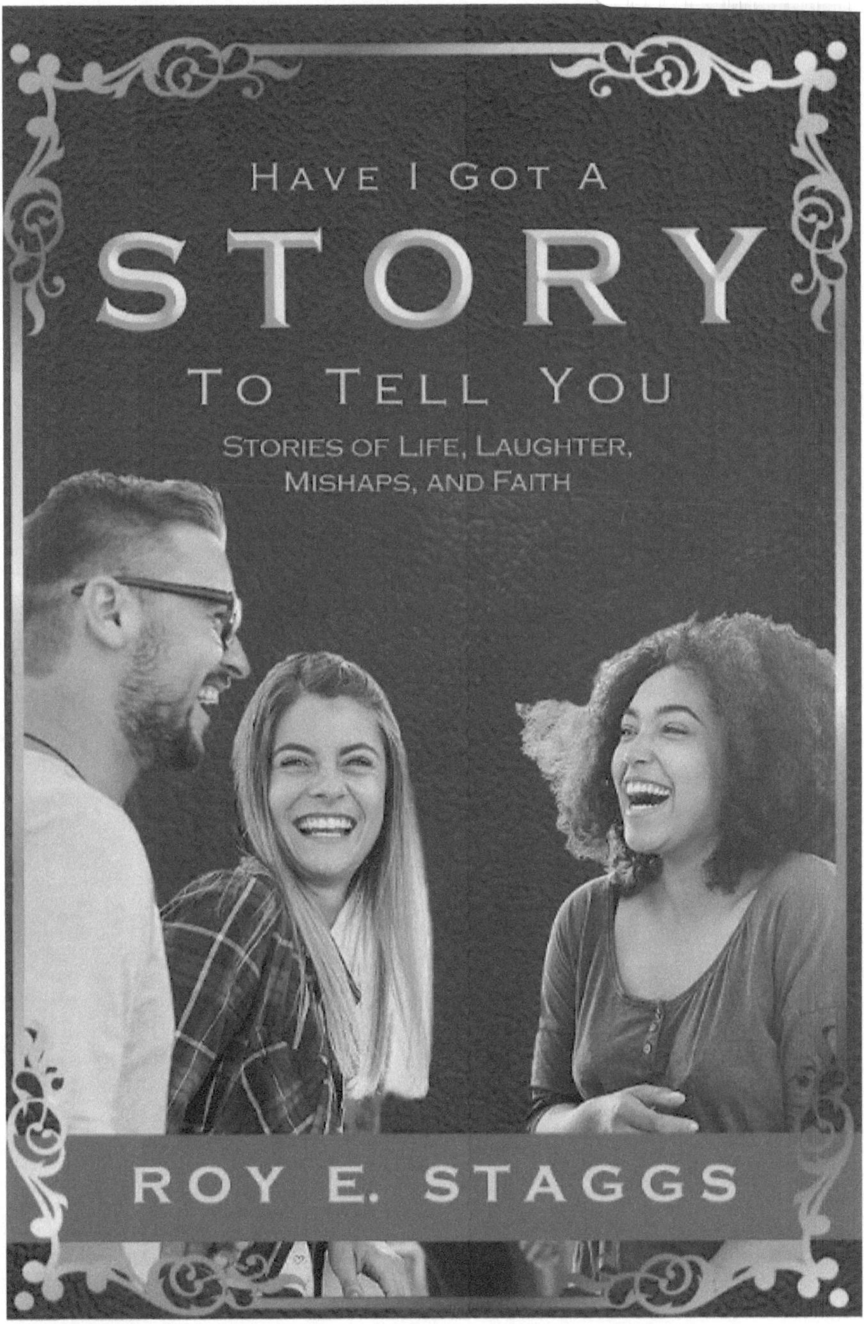

Stories of Life, Laughter, Mishaps, and Faith

ROY E. STAGGS

Have I Got A

Story

To Tell You

Stories of Life, Laughter, Mishaps, and Faith

ROY E. STAGGS

ISBN: 978-1-963565-14-0 (Paperback)

ISBN: 978-1-961677-98-2 (E-Book)

Library of Congress Control Number: 2024913811

Printed in the United States of America

Published by:

info@thequippyquill.com
(302) 295-2278

Acknowledgements

THE AUTHOR GRATEFULLY ACKNOWLEDGES THE FOLLOWING people for their contributions to the stories in this book.

Luther Runnels, former Fire Fighter, Fire Marshal, and EMT. Tyler Texas
Carol Staggs, Teacher, Lecturer, and Adjunct, Midland Texas
Robert Staggs, former Petty Officer, United States Navy, Clayton, Oklahoma

Table of Contents

Introduction

EVERY ACTION SOMEONE TAKES HAS A CONSEQUENCE WHETHER good, bad, or indifferent. Sometimes those consequences come back to haunt a person. Like the stories you are about to read, some actions are funny to some but not to others. Some actions occur by divine intervention, while others are created by man. Some of these stories will see the humor in some of the stories. Life is too short not to be unhappy. Everyone needs to laugh now and again. I have always heard that people who laugh a lot live longer. That endorphins thing is the reason. But, with laughter, life also brings tears of joy, sadness, fear, and faith. It is good the stop and look around yourself and see the individual trees in the forest. People also need quiet time to themselves to think. I remember watching some of the old-timers in my youth, sitting in a porch swing, daydreaming as if they didn't have a care in the world.

When I was a young man and all stressed out over some situation, I would go to my grandparents' house. They lived several miles from town, where it was peaceful and quiet. I would spend time just visiting and sitting in that old porch swing. I would often fall asleep on the front porch with a cool evening breeze blowing in my face. That was such a relaxing time. I would leave that place relaxed, destressed, and ready to face the world again. Of course, I enjoyed visiting with my grandparents and other family members.

There are times in life when we feel like God doesn't hear us or even care about us. We get ourselves into situations that bring about stress, discomfort, and nervous worrying, and get our stomachs in a knot. Our problems are many times brought about by our own actions or lack thereof. Then, we pray for relief but usually asking for the problem to be resolved our way. We don't consider how were got there in the first place. We tend to put God in a box and only take HIM out when we are in trouble or want something. Those wants are usually something we don't need but want them so badly. When God doesn't make them suddenly appear, we get mad and put God back in the box. Sometimes we need to get to ourselves, get quiet, sit down, and just listen. People would be surprised what they will hear.

People want things done today in a nano second. We are always in a hurry to get somewhere or do something. When someone gets in our way or doesn't move fast enough to suit our needs, we get angry. Someone once defined a nano second as the time it takes the light to turn green and the car behind you to honk the horn. I wondered just how much time we are wasting by doing this. Life is passing us by so fast, yet we want to live a hundred miles an hour. Again, life is short; enjoy it while you can.

Other times we see things, we try to apply some scientific explanation to the event. Miracles happen every day; we just don't realize it at the time. We see things we often don't want to believe, rather than taking things by faith. People often criticize others for believing in miracles and even believing in Christ. My dad used to say that we are judged by the scars we bare for Christ. If you are a believer, you are judged by mankind already as one of those Bible thumpers, a holy rollie, or simply a nut case. It takes all kinds of people to make a world. The believers are living in the world but aren't really a part of it. In this book, the readers will find stories of faith, read about miracles, laugh out loud at the funny stories, and perhaps even shed a tear when they read of how God intervened in the characters' lives.

The last words I have for the readers are being patient with yourself, being kind to others, taking time to stop and listen, and keeping a short prayer list. Relax and read the stories that will bring you joy, tears, laughter, and faith.

God Bless

Roy E. Staggs

Hank the Handyman

EVERY TOWN HAS ITS HANDY PEOPLE WHO FIX THINGS. SOME do it as a hobby, while others do it as a business. Our town was no different from any other one in this country. We had a handyman. His name was Hank. He was good at what he did, and he didn't charge an arm and a leg for his services. He worked a lot for the elderly and handicapped citizens. Hank would let those who were in unfortunate circumstances or down on their luck pay their bills over time. He was just an all-around decent guy.

Everyone in our town knew him. Hank was not married, and he still lived in his parents' home. Hank became the town hero when he saved two children's lives. He also kept his father alive after he had had a stroke and before the ambulance arrived. He was a special person indeed.

Hank grew up in our town, and he was a hometown boy. He was already an adult when my class graduated from high school. His parents convinced him to start a business when he was twenty-six years old. He had a full-time job, and he was a handyman on the side.

Two years later, his workload had doubled. Hank continued to work full-time, but he started a handyman business. He called it Hank's Handy Works. He even had business cards made and an ad printed in the Sunday paper. Some say that he made more money in his part-time work than in his full-time job.

Betty was a senior citizen who lived just down the street from Hank. She had known Hank since he was a child. She had been widowed when she was fifty. Her husband had had a heart attack and passed away on the same day. When Betty's dryer stopped working, she called Hank's parents and asked if Hank was available to repair it.

Hank stopped by on his lunch break to check out the dryer. The dryer had tripped an electrical breaker. No more than fifteen minutes later, Hank had repaired the dryer. Hank refused any pay for his service. He knew that she was on a fixed income. The widow dropped off a freshly baked apple pie at his house for his services.

Hank gladly accepted that pie in lieu of money. That was Hank all right. He was generous with his time and kindhearted.

He spent Saturdays working at his parents' home. He would mow the grass, trim the bushes, plant flowers, and do general maintenance. He worked well with his hands.

He spent Sundays in Sunday school and church. Hank did not work on Sundays. He rested from his labor. Sometimes if something broke, Hank would put a quick fix on it and do complete repairs the next day. Again, that was Hank.

Some people say that Hank had premonitions. He would be getting ready to go somewhere when an image would pop into his head. That image would be of someone he would meet a few minutes later. These premonitions also brought him to certain places at certain times. Some said that it was God guiding him to places where he needed to be when something was about to occur. No one knew for sure.

People only said this after the incidents. Others said that Hank must have been an angel sent from heaven. No one knew about that for sure either.

Most thought that he was just lucky and that he should have bought a lottery ticket or gone to Las Vegas. Everything Hank touched turned to gold. When he started his business, he took out an ad in the paper. The next day, he had eleven calls about repairs. As far as anyone knew, Hank never had a day when he wasn't doing something for someone.

Those so-called premonitions led Hank to places where most people didn't want to be. One day, he left for lunch fifteen minutes early. He arrived at a stoplight just in time to witness an automobile accident. When Hank got out of his truck, the car caught on fire. As he approached the automobile, he saw a lady sitting in the passenger seat. She was unconscious. Hank also noticed that she was about eight months pregnant. Hank forced open the door, took the lady from the car, and set her down in his truck. As he turned back, the car exploded. She had been the only occupant.

The other car had a drunken man in it. With all his strength, Hank forced the door open about the time a fire truck arrived. The man was alive and conscious. Hank directed the firefighter to his truck to attend to the pregnant lady. She was not seriously injured, and neither was her baby. Hank asked the firefighter not to mention his name. He didn't want to be a hero or have his picture in the paper.

Hank had other occurrences like that in his life. Was it luck, or was he led there by someone from above? No one knows, but two things for sure were that Hank was present and that someone's life was affected. Many people saw the things that were going on in Hank's life firsthand.

His parents were so proud of Hank and glad that he still lived at home. Now, Hank had the money to live on his own, but he wanted to live there to help his parents.

Hank was going to eat lunch at one of the local restaurants with his boss. They closed up shop, locked the door, and headed for his boss's vehicle. Hank stopped, turned around, and said, "I think I need to go home for a bit. I'll meet you at the café." Hank hurried home, and when he walked into his parents' house, his father fell to the floor. Hank tended to his father while his mother called for an ambulance. The doctors later revealed that Hank's father had had a stroke. His father made a full recovery. It was a miracle that Hank had been there; indeed, it was. The premonition thing had happened again, or had it just been luck that he had wanted to go home?

Hank got off work one Tuesday and drove to a house on the north side of town. He was supposed to look at replacing the wooden porch steps. When he pulled up into the driveway, he just sat there for a minute or two. The resident approached Hank's truck. Hank opened the door, got out, and looked across the street at an open garage door. The resident asked Hank what he was looking at. Hank replied, "I see one of those old refrigerators with locking handles. Kids can get in those things, but they can't get out."

Hank and the resident hurriedly ran across the street. They opened the old refrigerator door. Two small children were inside.

They were already turning blue. They pulled the children from the refrigerator and began mouth-to-mouth resuscitation. The resident who was helping Hank went inside the house, grabbed the phone from the mother, and called for an ambulance. The mother had been hysterically calling to find her children. She thought they had gone over to their friend's house. The two children survived. The ambulance driver told Hank and the resident, "It was a good thing you were here. In another minute to two, those two kids would have been statistics."

Hank just smiled and said, "Glad to see they are going to be OK."

Hank patted the ambulance attendant on the back and went back across the street.

All the newspapers reported the incident. The news personalities called Hank to interview him, but he refused. Hank's only comment was, "I would be afraid to take credit for something God did." Several people heard of Hank's premonitions. Many thought he was a fortune-teller. They falsely accused him of being from Satan.

Others quickly came to his rescue, quoting incidents where people's lives had been saved. At that time, Hank was a very unpopular man. Hank was an avid church attendee. He even taught Sunday school.

Who could ever think that he was from Satan? The rumor was that Hank did these things for gain. Hank never accepted a dime from anyone whom he helped. Those he helped wanted to repay him, but he refused.

Hank certainly had a dilemma on his hands. What would he do with his premonitions now? Would he continue to follow them, or would he now ignore them? Hank knew the answer, but he didn't tell anyone. Hank lived unaffected by things going around him, including the political structures in the city that he lived in. He went to work, helped others, and went home to be with his parents. Hank's life was full of joy and peace. It appeared that nothing fazed him. He was always happy, even when tragedy struck. He did what he was supposed to do, and he went on with life. Many people wished that they had the kind of peace that surrounded Hank.

Hank walked with a partial limp. When he had been six years old, he had contracted polio. His left leg experienced permanent

9

damage. This damage disqualified him from military service. Many places would not hire Hank because of this disability.

Hank didn't participate in sports while in high school due to his disability, but he could throw a baseball, straight and far. The baseball team comments on how far Hank could throw the ball, but they knew he couldn't run like they could. None of the sports teams wanted Hank on their team but Hank understood that his disability prevented him from being a good player. Hank wasn't discouraged about his disability or inability to play sports so he concentrated on his grades instead. They were excellent according to his teachers.

When Hank had finished high school, he had been offered a scholarship for college, but he had refused it. He just wanted to go to work. No one knows for sure, but most people think that he wanted to stay close to home to help his mother and father.

One thing everyone can say positive about Hanks high school years, other than his grades, was his IQ. In Hank's freshman year of high school, they had tested his IQ. His score of 150 surprised everyone, including his teachers. Hank was a person whom not many people understood concerning his intelligence. This intelligence rating put Hank on the spot in some of his classes. The other classmates thought of him as someone with a slow learning capacity, until they saw the honor roll postings each semester. I do believe they were impressed but also jealous of his ability to make good grades.

Hank's father was a disabled veteran from the Korean War. He had earned an early pension from the government. His mother waited tables at the local café and took in sewing for extra money. Hank also helped by mowing lawns on the weekends while he was in high school. The household didn't earn a great deal of money, but they could buy the things that they needed. They lived in an old house that had been given to them by Hank's grandparents. The house was debt free, and this helped considerably. Hank knew the meaning of struggle by the time he was in elementary school.

After Hank graduated from high school, he went to work in a hardware store. As time went on, this made it easy for him to purchase parts for his handyman jobs. He eventually created an open account at his place of employment. The owner settled his account at the end of each month. The owner was happy to do that for Hank because he worked on the side for the owner. It was a good working arrangement for Hank and his employer. Hank's boss said that he brought business into the store when he told them to buy certain things for their houses. Hank was not a salesman, but people took his advice.

Hank also chose not to marry. He did have a girlfriend, but Hank didn't think it was fair for him to marry her. Hank knew his childhood illnesses caused him to be unable to father children and Hank knew that his girlfriend would want children if they married. Hank used to say that no marriage was complete without children. Everyone, excluding Hank's girlfriend, thought adoption was a good substitute. Hank's girlfriend wanted children of her own. Hank couldn't provide that, so she left and moved on to someone else. Hank was a very understanding person, but his mother saw his grief. He would never be a parent, had a disability, and felt that no one wanted him. One day, Hank had an experience that changed his life forever.

When he was twenty-one years old, he was awakened in the middle of the night by a dream. He saw a vision of a child lost in the woods. He rose from his bed, got dressed, and drove to the police station.

When he arrived, a police officer was exiting the building. The man was clearly upset and crying. Hank asked the distraught man if he could help him. He told Hank that his daughter was missing. She had wandered off, and she was lost in the woods.

Hank said, "I saw her in my dreams. Let me help you find her."

The man thought that Hank was trying to impress others, but he would have done anything to find his child. Other people had been searching for hours. When it had become dark, they had gone into a panic. The fire department, the police department, and many friends had been out combing the woods for the child, but to no avail. The child's mother and neighbors were still frantically looking for the little girl. Hank took the man to his truck and drove toward a patch of woods near the child's home. The two got out with their flashlights and walked into the wooded area. Hank went one way, and the man went the other to search for the child. Hank found the little girl sitting on a five-gallon bucket and crying for her mother and father. Hank quickly picked up the little girl and carried her to his truck. Hank screamed out the father's name, saying, "Don, I found her. Come to the truck."
The little girl looked at Hank and said, "I saw you in a dream last night. When I was lost, something told me to sit on that bucket, and you would find me." From that moment on, Hank knew that he had a gift. His children were everyone else's children. He didn't need to be a biological parent.

Hank went on with his life as if he knew his destiny. He would be the handyman with a special gift that no one understood. Hank and his parents knew all too well that he had been special from birth. Hank was not supposed to live when he was born. The doctors said that his mind wouldn't develop beyond the age of six or seven. Obviously, they were wrong. Hank developed as any normal child would. His mind was as sharp as a tack and above normal for his age. Yes, Hank was a special gift.

As an adult, one of Hank's contributions to his church was to volunteer for youth camp. He would go every summer with the group as an adult supervisor. He also taught his usual lessons from the Bible at camp. Hank's contributions were enormous. He drove a church bus, did activities with the groups, read Bible stories to the children every night, and even helped cook meals. Hank was a natural, and all the kids loved him. After camp was over, he helped clean up the church bus and organized the next year's camp program.

Hank had one more contribution to his community. He helped Boy Scouts learn how to braid ropes, tie knots, set up a campsite, build a fire, and do many more things. One summer, he went to Boy Scout camp with the local troop. He was a genuine success story. Hank read stories at that camp also. The boys liked Hank and wanted him to be their scoutmaster, but he refused. He already had too much on his plate. He would drop by now and then to help the boys with their lessons.

After Hank went to work full-time, they could afford to eat at a local café where his mother worked. Every Sunday after church, most of the people went to one of three restaurants to eat lunch. Hank and his parents were no different.

This particular Sunday, Hank and his parents went to another restaurant. Hank made a last-minute decision. His mother objected, but his dad said that they needed to try something different for a change. Hank and his parents had finished their lunch and ordered dessert. The restaurant was crowded and noisy. They saw other people there from their church, as well as other friends.

Suddenly, Hank heard a commotion at a table behind him. Hank jumped up and went to see what was going on. He saw a mother with three children at a table. The mother was trying to dislodge food from her child's throat. The child was already turning blue. Hank grabbed the child and did the Heimlich maneuver. A piece of meat flew out of the child's mouth. Hank stood by while the mother comforted the child. This mother had been one of the people who had thought that Hank was evil and that his gift was from Satan. Hank smiled, patted the child's back, and went back to his table.

Three days later, Hank received a letter in the mail. Hank read it. It was a thank-you letter. There was no return address on the envelope, but Hank knew whom the letter was from. Again, Hank was at the right place at the right time. Was this luck or another miracle? One thing for sure was that the child's mother never said another thing against Hank for the rest of her life.

When Hank was forty-five years old, his father passed away. His mother died a year later. Hank was all alone now. The old house that he lived in was so quiet. The sounds of his father's western movies playing on the television were now gone. He no longer heard his mother's voice, saying, "Supper is ready, boys." It would take a few years for Hank to get used to his parents being gone. His sadness only became worse when he did things for others.

Hank continued to work until he was sixty years old. He was still a strong and healthy man at that age. He was still working at the hardware store. The owner had passed away when Hank was forty-three. In his will, the owner gave Hank the hardware store and his assets.

Hank kept the business open and hired the man who had helped him save the two children who had been locked in the refrigerator. The man had spent twenty years working at an auto manufacturer in their parts room, but he had been laid off due to budget cuts. They made a good team. Hank also hired a part-time worker to help out on Saturdays and afternoons. Hank continued doing his handyman job.

His workload increased due to the hours that he spent at his new position at the hardware business. One Monday morning, Hank didn't show up for work. Calls to his home went unanswered for two hours. Finally, Hank's coworker asked the police to go by Hank's house to check on him. Upon arriving, they found Hank in his bed with his hands crossed and a smile on his face. He was dead. The coroner determined that Hank died peacefully in his sleep.

The church was not large enough to seat everyone at Hank's funeral, so they set up chairs under in a large tent. There were still people who had to stand. After Hank's funeral, a man with an envelope walked up to Hank's business employee. Hank had signed his will three days earlier, giving him his hardware and handyman business. A new sign was constructed above the door of the business. The sign read, "Hank's Handy Hardware Store."

Pictures of Hank still hang on the wall of the store. Hank's old house was torn down, and the one-acre lot was given to charity to sell at auction. The money in Hank's personal bank account was given to his church to help the youth group.

Hank affected the lives of many people in that small town. His memory is everywhere. A park was renamed Hank's Corner in his honor. Once a year, thirty-three children gather at Hank's Corner to celebrate Hank's life. He touched so many people. He was sometimes criticized by people for his lack of friends. He was scorned by those who didn't understand him. He was loved by those whose lives he touched. Hank's life had been full of mystery. He suffered at the hands of an illness in his youth. He endured polio. He lost a girlfriend because he could not father children. He was accused after he found the child in the woods. The authorities cleared him after the child had given a statement. God uses people to do *His* work. Hank endured. He was blessed with a gift that no person but God understood.

By the way, Hank's old girlfriend named her last child after Hank. She and her husband divorced after ten years of marriage. She lived with her parents until their passing. She is one of the persons who organized the celebrations and renaming of the park. She sits in the same pew that Hank sat in at church. I think she misses him, and we do too. God bless you.

A Day at the Beach

(Based on a True Story)

BOBBY'S MOTHER AND FATHER HAD DIVORCED A YEAR OR SO earlier. The burden of feeding the two children who were still at home was evident. Bobby worked after school and on weekends to earn money so that he could support himself and relieve his mother's burdens.

Bobby had two older brothers. One was already living on his own. He spent time with that brother when he could. The older brother had a disability and a mad idea of going to the big city. He could go to work and live on his own. The younger brother was still struggling with a decision. He felt that he was a burden to his mother. He did go and live with his uncle for a while, but his mother wanted him back home. The only other way to not burden anyone was by joining the military.

None of this compared to a later event that would change his life in ways that no one could understand. By this time, he was only seventeen. He was a senior in high school but cutting classes to hang out with his friends and work.

He had been a good student until the divorce. His father had left, taking his personal belongings and the money in the bank account. What a dilemma it had been.

He would turn eighteen that September. After he graduated from his school, he could go to work full-time and earn enough money to live on. But time was running out for his mother. She had no job or way to sustain herself.

He wanted to join the military that summer before he turned eighteen. He could designate money to be sent home to his mother if she needed help. Somehow, he persuaded his mother and father to sign the papers so that he could join the military. This would be a decision of a lifetime. Life would change for him in ways that he could never imagine. Things would happen, but he would overcome.

His brother took him to the recruitment center at five o'clock that Saturday morning. He boarded a bus to the airport and then a plane to boot camp. He was a navy man now. He spent boot camp in Orlando, Florida. The weather was wonderful, and there were many sights to see and things to do.

After boot camp ended, he was off to Accession School, commonly called "A" School. The school was located on a large base divided by an interstate highway in Tennessee. It took a while to find his way around, but he managed. After "A" school, he was sent to Jacksonville to board the USS *Enterprise*. It would have been a good adventure, but lack of proper training on the flight deck spoiled that tour.

He was deferred to Japan, but he didn't want to go there. After some finagling with a buddy, his orders were changed. He received new orders to report to the naval air station in Corpus Christi, Texas.

While there, he was in comfortable surroundings. His family had moved from the area a few years earlier but other family members had remained in the area. Many relatives lived within a seventy-mile radius of the base. Life was good there. He made new friends and enjoyed military life at that point, although he didn't particularly care for the bureaucracy.

The military life is unlike any other. Many misfortunes can befall those who are in the military if they don't follow the rules set forth in military policies and procedures. The soldier—rather sailor in this case—must be vigilant and keep his or her mind on the matters at hand to avoid the pitfalls. So many times, some have been sidetracked and ended up in trouble with civilian authority. This is something the military does not like and there is punishment from both sides, civilian and military. Once the civilian authority is finished dealing with the military person, the military takes over and dishes out their own punishment to the person. Kind of puts an new light on that double jeopardy thing doesn't it? He was now twenty years old and in his second year of enlistment.

The navy always taught and trained, especially how to swim. If someone was on the water, it was a good idea to know how to swim. He did just that. They had constant inspections of their barracks and uniforms, daily exercise, and of course, a job to do. Each person in the military had a job in their field of expertise to do. Some were guards, some fueled aircrafts, some flew aircraft, some worked in maintenance, some cooked in the chow hall, and so on. All enlisted personnel had to do guard duty on the rotating basis. Every day there was something to do and get done to keep the military machine properly oiled, fueled, and trained.

He spent time with his fellow sailors seeing the sights and visiting off-limits places that the guys got to while in the military. He didn't like those places, but he went to appease his friends. A weekend at the beach was the thing that most military personnel who were stationed near an ocean enjoyed. This ocean happened to be the Gulf of Mexico and Corpus Christi Bay. Padre Island was a great place for beachgoers who came from all over the South, especially Texas. High schoolers and college students found this place to be accommodating and fun during Spring Break. The weather was good unless a hurricane was in the Gulf of Mexico.

It was a hot summer day on that Saturday afternoon when some of the sailors from the base gathered at the beach. The sailors went to Padre Island, bringing food and drinks with them. Sailors would spend the day and sometimes the night on the beach. They built a fire on the beach, and they were having a good time. They cooked over the fire, had a few drinks, swam in the ocean, and hung out for a day of leisure. They were away from the base, military discipline, and duty. They enjoyed every minute away from the base. This was a good stress reliever for the sailors in Corpus Christi.

There were a lot of people at the beach that day: girls, surfers, casual beachcombers, and families. There were even people looking for souvenirs on the beach with metal detectors. There was always something to do on the sandy beaches of Padre Island. The water was perfect, and there was a light coastal breeze. In fact, there was always a breeze blowing on the coast.

Sunscreen was the ritual for everyone on the beach, and the navy man was no exception. He applied his usual sunscreen and asked one of the girls to apply some of it on his back. He was a good-looking young man, so the girls were accommodating. The navy man didn't mind either. One could say it was a mutual exchange. He would return the favor if requested to do so.

Almost everyone swam in the warm Gulf's waters. The swimmer could go out a hundred feet and still be able to touch the bottom. Other places dropped off a little more, so one had to be careful not to get in over one's head. No one thought about the sharks, except those who were fishing for them on the piers. Everyone knew that they were in the ocean, but not many people paid it any mind while in the shallow waters off the island. The people were busy having fun, swimming, and playing in the water. Other people were lying on the beach to get a tan. It was certainly a bathing suit kind of day on the beach.

The navy man went into the water and swam around for a while. Most of the time, he could touch the bottom. Looking around, he could see others in his area. He floated around, swam some, and then floated some more. It wasn't long before he was about a hundred yards out in the water. That was a little too far for safety's sake. So like any person of reasonable sense, he began to swim back toward shore.

Although he was a good swimmer, the farther out a person was, the harder it was to swim back to shore. It seemed like the harder he swam, the further out he got. He was swimming hard, but getting nowhere. The ocean waters were trying to carry him out to sea, but the navy man was resisting furiously. He tried and tried to get closer to shallow waters, but he couldn't. Even though he was a good swimmer, he wished that he had a lifejacket. No one wore a lifejacket at the beach. That would get in the way. He kept on swimming and trying to reach shallow water. The more he swam, the more aware he became that he was in deep trouble.

The navy man went under after several minutes of struggle. He came back up, bobbing like a cork in the water. He kept trying to swim, but the current was too strong, and he was so tired. He knew that he had to keep trying to get to shallow waters. His life now depended on it. As he struggled, he went down a second time. Thoughts flashed in his mind, his heart beat furiously, and his pulse raced as if he were running a marathon. In a way, he was in a marathon—for his life. He thought that it was all over for him. He would leave behind two brothers, his mother, and his father. Uncles, aunts, and cousins would grieve over the loss alongside his family. He just knew it was all over.

The navy man bobbled up again from the Gulf's waters. He vacuumed in a deep breath just before he sank into the deep waters for the last time. As the navy man went under, he raised his hand toward heaven in a last-ditch effort that someone might see him going down. The navy would undoubtedly miss him at morning roll call, as would the two buddies he came to the beach with.

They looked around, but they couldn't find him. He was supposed to be in the shallows. They had come back to shore to flirt with some of the girls, and they thought their fellow sailor had been right behind them. They scanned the horizon but couldn't see anything. Past a certain point, the reflection of the sun on the water blocked any view of a person in the water.

It didn't take long for a person to get into trouble in the ocean. Those waters cold be treacherous. The undertow was something to watch for, along with sharks. Jellyfish were also something to be on guard for. There were many other dangers to watch out for. The worst one was drifting out to sea. Many people drowned in the Gulf's waters by drifting out too far and being unable to swim back to shore.

As the navy man went down for the last time, he felt a hand grab his. A surfer had seen him drifting out and had paddled to him as he was going down the first time. The navy man had no idea that the surfer was close to him. He saw that surfers were farther out in the water, but the waves were not so great for surfing. The surfer pulled the navy man up on his board, and they paddled to shallow water.

The sailor was grateful that the surfer had been out there. He thanked him all the way back to shore. I cannot imagine the thoughts that were going through the navy man's mind when he was going down for the last time in the rolling waters of the gulf. It must have been an indescribable moment.

Later, he said that life flashed before a people when they thought that they would die. He certainly thought his life was over when he went under for the last time. The surfer was grateful that he had seen the navy man's hand reaching toward heaven.

The sailor didn't go back into the waters that day. His fun and swimming were all over. All he wanted to do was hang out on the beach. The surfer went back into the water for more casual surfing.

He went back to the beach many times after that event. He stayed close to the shore and in the shallow waters. The memory was just too much to forget.

God had spared the navy man's life that day in the waters off Padre Island. God had a plan for everyone, and he certainly was not finished with the navy man. Sometimes it takes the Gulf's waters to get someone's attention to that fact. The navy man serves the Lord to this day. He faced happy times and tragic events in his life after that day. He held steadfast to his belief in Jesus Christ and made it a habit to read his Bible daily.

A good lesson was learned that day. It is wise to be aware of how far out one is when swimming in the ocean. The waters can be luring and persuasive, but the consequences can be fatal. It is wise to use the buddy system; always swim in pairs or perhaps in threes.

I am grateful for God's hand rescuing the sailor by way of the surfer that day. God uses people to do his miracles and help his people. Many times, we get so involved with life that we fail to see how far away from God we are. Will a surfer be waiting nearby when you go under? I know what people are thinking when they read this story. They say that it is just a way to get people to believe in miracles. Perhaps it is a way to scare people away from the beach.

My duty in life is to be a witness and not to judge, persuade, or convince anyone of anything. My duty is just to testify and let others make their own decisions. It's their life and their decision. There is one last thing to share. I know this story is true. The navy man is my brother, and I love him so.

Eyes and Boats

BILLY JOE WAS JUST AN ORDINARY GUY. ONE OF HIS FISHING trips was about to bring some serious doubts on his ability to pick a good fishing spot for the weekend. The excitement of what occurred is still the talk of the town. "Sink or swim" was the motto that he left behind because of this ill-fated trip.

Billy Joe had a wife, three kids, and a job that paid the bills most of the time. Overtime was a common occurrence for Billy Joe. His job required him to work every fourth Saturday. After the kids became teenagers, his wife started working at the local grocery store. Betty Jo enjoyed her job and life. Both Billy Joe and Betty Jo were happy with their suburban life.

Now Betty Jo attended a girl's night out once a month. She and her friends would take turns hosting a small get-together at their homes. The first order of business was to eat at a local restaurant and then go to one of their houses to play games or watch a movie.

Twice a year, Betty Jo and her friends would go to Las Vegas for a three-day weekend. They didn't gamble much, but they loved the shopping, sightseeing, and excursions. They had a blast on each trip.

Billy Joe felt about the same when he and his friends went hunting and fishing. While the wives were eating out and hosting a get-together, the husbands did the same. They played penny-ante poker was once a month, usually on a Saturday. None of the husbands or wives consumed alcohol or drugs. The girls had Diet Cokes, and regular Cokes; Dr. Pepper, or Pepsi were the drinks of the night for the guys.

When the wives went to Vegas, the boys went on weekend fishing or hunting trips. They were usually successful in catching fish and game most of the time. Fish, venison, dove, quail, elk, or other meats were always in their freezers. Twice a year, the husbands hosted a barbecue in the backyard. Plenty of food was cooked, and the eight or ten guests left full and happy. That was the way it was in their town and with their families: just good friends getting together for enjoyable fun. There were games, food, and laughter. Plenty of Coke, Diet Coke, Dr. Pepper, Pepsi, iced tea, and coffee were available for the guests.

It was Billy Joe's turn to plan the next fishing trip. He had been talking to some of his coworkers about different places to fish. One employee told of a place in East Texas where he had caught several ten- and twenty-pound catfish on trout lines. It was a very remote fishing lake deep in the Piney woods, and not many people knew about the lake. Perhaps the locals knew, but the word hadn't gotten out much. Some monster fish lived in those waters.

Billy Joe inquired about the location of the lake and how to get permission to go there. The coworker told Billy Joe about a man who owned property on the lake and charged fifty dollars per person for a three-day weekend. The property had a boat dock and a small cabin with bunks, electricity, and running water. Although the price seemed a little cheap, Billy Joe agreed it would be an inexpensive fishing trip for the guys.

Arrangements were made to rent the cabin for the weekend, and all four guys agreed it would be worth their time to check it out. Two weeks later, the four guys loaded up their gear, the boat, food, and supplies. The guys left Friday afternoon for the two-hour drive to the lake. Upon arriving, they unloaded everything, launched the boat, and set up for a night of trout-line fishing.

They set out four lines just before dark. They put bait on each line that would catch huge catfish. So far, they had experienced no problems. They were excited to take in their yield later that night. The guys went to the cabin, ate supper, and rested for the night's fishing expedition.

At about nine o'clock that night, the four men decided it was time to check their lines and retrieve their caught fish. They loaded themselves into a fourteen-foot flat-bottom boat and proceeded to the first line. Repeat?

Lights mounted on the front of the boat shown into the waters as the first guy pulled up a line. Three medium-sized catfish were taken from the line. The bait was replaced, and the line was put back into the water. The next line didn't yield any fish. They thought that the third line would have to be the one. No fish were found on the third line. Then they thought the fourth would have to be the golden line.

As they approached the fourth line's tie point, one man leaned over the front of the boat. He did this to grab a tree limb and prevent the boat from slamming into a willow tree. As the boat came to an abrupt halt, the tree limb swayed at the force being used to stop the boat. At that exact moment, something fell into the boat. One guy thought he dropped something. When he shone his flashlight, they saw that a cotton mouth was in the boat.

Every man scrambled to the back of the boat. This movement caused the willow tree's limb to sway again. Three more snakes dropped into the boat. About that time, Billy Joe pulled out his .22 handgun to shoot the snakes.

"You can't do that," one man exclaimed. "You're going to shoot a hole in the boat." It was too late. Billy Joe fired four shots at the snakes. He hit all four snakes.

"That was good shooting," one of the men shouted, "but the boat is leaking now."

Billy Joe had hit all four snakes, but the bullets had gone through the snakes and the bottom of the boat. When one of the men shone his flashlight up into the tree, all he could see were eyes looking back at them. All along the shoreline, the guys could see nothing but eyes looking back at them. At this point, the men were terrified.

Billy Joe steered the boat back to the boat dock. When they arrived, each shone their lights on the docks to detect snakes. Eyes looked back at them from there also. Billy Joe fired three more shots at the snakes. The eyes disappeared from the dock, and all four men exited the boat. Billy Joe secured the boat, and all four went directly back to the cabin.

Billy Joe shouted, "I never saw so many snakes in one place in all my life. Those water moccasins were everywhere. I don't like this place. I am ready to go home."

They waited until daylight before making a move toward the boat.

Billy Joe and one other man went to the dock early the next morning and loaded the boat. All four agreed that the trip was a disaster. No one wanted to go back into the water after their lines or even spend another night on that lake.

The boys left the lake and went back home. They managed to repair the boat the next day and vowed never to discuss that trip with anyone. Except for Billy Joe's coworker, no one else knew about the fishing trip's location.

Their wives came home Sunday night and inquired about the fishing trip. Billy Joe said, "Well, it wasn't that good. We didn't catch much. Guess we went there on an off day. Sometimes the fish just don't bite, and we just happened to be there when they didn't." The wives had had a great time in Vegas, but they were glad to be home.

The following Monday morning, Billy Joe saw the coworker who had talked about the lake with lots of fish. The coworker approached Billy Joe and asked about the trip. The coworker began to laugh and asked, "Did you guys catch very many snakes? Oh, I mean fish."

Billy Joe was furious. "Did you know about the snakes in the willow trees on that lake?"

The coworker answered, "No. I just heard about them from my uncle, who owned the cabin."

The coworker told the snake and fish story all around the factory, and everyone had a good laugh about the trip. Time would eventually heal all wounds concerning the fishing trip, and life went on for the fishing partners. Never again would they rely on the words of a coworker about places to fish.

Billy Joe traded in his flat-bottom boat and bought a bass boat. The four guys enjoyed using that boat to go on fishing trips to large lakes that were listed in fishermen's magazines.

Three months after Billy Joe had purchased his boat, he caught the record-breaking bass on a Texas lake. His picture was in a magazine, and all of Billy Joe's coworkers commented on his picture.

He was a hero at work, but the snake story came up repeatedly as Billy Joe received more attention for his fishing trips. It appeared that the snake story would never go away. There had to be a way to put it behind them.

One Friday afternoon, the coworker's uncle came to visit. The uncle toured the factory, and he was reintroduced to Billy Joe. The two began to talk. The uncle mentioned his escapades on the lake.

One of the stories was particularly interesting to Billy Joe. The uncle talked about a fishing trip that his nephew had taken with two of his friends on the lake. Everyone laughed when they heard that the coworker had shot five holes in his boat and that it had sunk in the lake before he could get back to the boat dock. The boat is still at the bottom of the lake. Although no one had been harmed by the incident, the coworker's friends had refused to talk to him again. The boat had belonged to one of the coworker's friends. He had lost all his gear plus the boat.

Billy Joe was excited to tell the story at the factory the next day to all his coworkers and friends. This story would top anything that had gone wrong on Billy Joe's trip for sure. The coworker quietly asked Billy Joe if they could call a truce, and Billy Joe agreed. Never again would there be any fishing trip discussions with coworkers at the factory. There were discussions about how many bullet holes it took to sink a boat. The answer was simple. It depended on how far the boat was away from the shore and the caliber of the gun.

You see, the coworker was deadly afraid of snakes and other creepy-crawly things. He also carried a .357 Magnum pistol on all his trips because he was a reserve deputy sheriff. When the coworker had fired those shots, each hole was about one inch in diameter. It didn't take many holes to sink a flat-bottom boat. The coworker had learned a lesson.

Billy Joe and his friends still fish on area lakes but during daylight hours. They haven't been on a night fishing trip since the snake incident.

The coworker hasn't fished since his snake experience because he is terrified of the water and things that swim in it. The coworker was laid off from the factory. He now owns and operates his own boat-repair business. He specializes in plugging bullet holes in aluminum boats, especially those from gunshots.

Billy Joe still works at the factory. He is now a shift supervisor and continues to fish and barbecue with his friends. The state decided to develop a large lake, which encompassed the smaller snake lake. This new lake is now a favorite fishing spot for Billy Joe and his friends during the daylight hours.

Betty Jo and her friends started a janitorial business. They clean commercial businesses and fishing cabins on the new lake. The coworker's uncle built thirty cabins on the new lake and hired Betty Jo to clean them. As for the snakes, they were displaced or killed during the construction of the new lake. Sometimes people report seeing eyes looking back at them from the small willow trees that line one of the lakeshore's sections.

Billy Joe, his wife, his friends, and their wives have never been to the lake at night. The wives never go there at night, especially after hearing the old uncle's snake story. The wives heard the snake and fishing story at the beauty parlor a week after it happened. It just goes to show that there are no secrets. Someone else always knows. God bless them all.

A Good Hat

HE WAS ABOUT THIRTY YEARS OLD WHEN HE WALKED INTO THE lottery commission's office. He strutted up to the counter like he had the world by the tail. He filled out the appropriate forms and handed them to the lady. The lady asked him to scan his ticket. The scanner revealed what he had seen when he scratched off the numbers on his ticket: He had won $1 million. After settling the income tax burdens, he ended up with about $700,000 in his bank account. That was one of the best moments of his life. The second, third, and fourth would come in about three months.

He was wise with his money. He invested much of it in safe securities using an investment firm. He also took his tax accountant's advice on managing his money and ended up owing IRS nothing when tax time came. In fact, he would receive a sizeable tax return, much to the Internal Revenue Service's dismay.

The first thing he did with his money was pay off all the debts that he and his wife had accumulated. They were thirty years old and debt free. They both drove older vehicles but decided to trade them in and pay off the difference to remain debt free. Their financial advisor wanted them to finance the purchase and improve their credit ratings, but Joe and his wife, Delores, disagreed. They had credit cards that they used frequently, and now, they would pay them off at the end of each month. This financing would build their credit ratings over time.

Delores purchased a new SUV with all the trim and customs that she wanted. Joe chose to keep his older truck. He had the outside painted and the interior repaired. They had now accomplished three of the four things that they set out to achieve. They paid off their debts, they purchased Delores a new vehicle, and Joe refurbished his old truck. The fourth would come a month later.

Joe was not a spendthrift, and Delores wasn't one either. They lived in an older house on thirty acres of land. Joe had inherited the house from his parents. One could say that Joe was a cowboy at heart. Joe and Delores had a small ranching operation or hobby ranching as it was called. They had full-time jobs in the city, but they were always raising a few head of cattle and some chickens. They had two dogs that kept watch over their property while they were at work. It was a dream life for Joe and Delores.

Joe had always wanted a custom-made cowboy hat. They cost between $600 and $3,000, depending on the hat. Joe was not about to spend $3,000, but he was ready to buy a custom-made hat because of his recent winnings. He was willing to spend a maximum of $1,000. Delores agreed that it would be the right thing to do. They were planning on attending the National Finals Rodeo later that year.

They made the trip to a custom hatmakers shop and began to look around. The owner was a great hatmaker. He had a reputation of looking at a person and making a hat to fit that customer's face to perfection. He made hats for entertainers on occasion. Joe was impressed with his talents. Joe sat down, and the hatmaker took a few photographs: front, back, and each side. The hatmaker put several hats on Joe. After being measured, being photographed, and reviewing several hats, they decided on a design. The custom-made, $1,000 hat would be ready in three months.

Joe and Delores went about their business as they patiently waited for the hat. They made their reservations for the National Finals

Rodeo, hotels, excursions, and other things that they could now afford. It would be a treat for them.

Time went by. Then one day, there it was: the email for his completed custom-made hat. Off they went to pick up the hat. It was a perfect match for Joe's face. Delores loved it. The hatmaker took photographs of Joe with his new hat on to use for advertising his talents. The day finally came to leave for the Rodeo. They boarded the plane, took their seats, and off they went. They sat three rows from the front of the plane. Joe was in the aisle seat, and Delores was in the window seat. The middle seat was open, so they placed their iPads, phones, and Joe's new hat there.

The plane made one stop on their journey to the Rodeo, but they did not have to change planes. Joe and Delores went to the restroom while waiting and then returned to their seats. Delores took off her jacket and placed it in the middle seat. As new passengers boarded the plane, a young lady wanted the middle seat. Joe relented and stood up. The lady almost jumped into the seat. Joe barely had time to move his hat. It was a close call for Joe's $1,000 hat.

Joe and Delores arrived in Las Vegas and caught a cab to their hotel. They checked in and unloaded their luggage. Joe took off his hat. Delores threw her bags on the bed, narrowly missing Joe's new hat. It was another close call.

Joe and Delores decided to eat dinner at an upscale steak restaurant. They were seated at a table for four. Joe set his hat in one of the vacant chairs, watching it carefully to ensure the hat's safety. They enjoyed a glass of tea and of water, a salad, and a nice Fort Worth rib eye. The waitperson came by frequently to bring more water and tea.

On one trip, the waitperson reached for Joe's glass of tea. As she did this, she accidentally tipped the pitcher over and filled Joe's new, custom-made hat full of tea.

Joe quickly grabbed his precious hat and ran for the restroom. He emptied the tea from his hat and grabbed loads of paper towels to dry the hat. A gentleman came forward with a towel and a hairdryer to help dry the hat. The kind gentleman said, "You can say one thing for your hat. It must be a quality hat because it didn't leak a drop between the table and the restroom."

Joe was furious. When he returned to the table, Delores was dealing with the waitperson regarding the incident. The restaurant offered to have the hat cleaned at its expense. Joe wasn't having any of that. He sent a text to his hatmaker inquiring about possible damage to his hat. The hatmaker informed Joe that he should bring it to him when he returned. Then they would check it out. The restaurant further agreed to delay cleaning the hat until Joe could get the hat examined.

Joe and Delores left the restaurant. They had not had to pay for their meal. One of the cowboys, who happened to be in the restaurant, had informed Joe that his hat could be salvaged. That comment helped Joe's attitude a little. Joe took his hat to the room while Delores sat at a casino table. Joe came down later, leaving his hat in the room.

Joe and Delores attended the opening night at the rodeo. They were in box seats—compliments of the hotel. As they sat there enjoying the Rodeo, a drunken man almost sat on Joe's hat. As Joe and the man reached for the hat simultaneously, the man spilled beer on the brim, and some went inside the hat.

Joe quickly got up and went to find someone who could clean his hat. He found someone. The man cleaned up Joe's hat. It took quite a while before the man could get the beer smell out of the hat, but he finally did. Joe wasn't happy, but at least the hat could be salvaged. Joe and Delores had a great time at the rodeo. They even went on a couple of excursions during the day. After a few days, it was time to catch a plane home.

Joe and Delores boarded the plane and sat in the third row from the front of the airplane. Joe sat in the aisle seat, and Delores sat in the window seat. The plane was full, so eventually, they had to give up the middle seat to a very talkative cowgirl. She admired Joe's hat and carried on a lengthy conversation with Delores constantly during their flight.

On the way home from the airport, Joe and Delores decided to stop at the hatmaker's place of business. Joe handed the hat to the hatmaker. He quickly examined it and set it down on his counter while he retrieved some hat cleaner. Joe picked up the hat and took one last look at it.

While the hatmaker talked to another customer, Joe sat down in a chair, and Delores looked around the store. Joe set his hat in the adjacent chair with a watchful eye. A man came up to the counter and called for the hatmaker. The man saw that he was busy, so he hung around the counter. Delores brought a jacket to Joe and asked him to try it on. Joe stood up, took off his jacket, and put on the new one. It fit perfectly. The man at the counter turned around to admire the jacket. He took one step forward, stumbled, and fell on top of Joe's hat. All Joe heard was a crunching sound. When the rather large man stood up, the hat was as flat as a pancake.

The hatmaker returned and asked for Joe's hat. With cleaner in hand, he grabbed Joe's hat. "What happened? I thought you spilled tea in the hat. This hat is ruined. Who did this?"

The large intoxicated man spoke up and offered to pay for the hat.

The hatmaker said, "You couldn't pay for a hatband much less a $1,000 hat." The intoxicated man was well known around the store as he often showed up to look at merchandise he couldn't possible afford. The intoxicated man would try on hats and other western apparel but couldn't afford anything in this store.

The large man stood there in astonishment. "It's $1,000 hat? Who would pay that much for a hat?"

Joe stood face-to-face with the large man and said, "I would, and I did. That is my hat."

Joe was beside himself. All these years, he had wanted a custom-made hat. When he had finally got one, it had been one problem after another. Someone had almost sat on it once on the plane and once at the Rodeo. Someone had spilled tea in his hat at the restaurant. Now someone had actually sat on it. Joe felt as if he wasn't supposed to have a custom-made hat. He was very disappointed. Joe handed the hat to the hatmaker, and he and Delores went home to morn and await the hat maker's decision. Joe just loved that hat and to see it in that condition was almost unbearable.

About a month later, Joe received a call from the hatmaker. "Joe," the man said, "I believe we have your hat in good condition now. It looks better than it did when you first picked it up."

Joe was just beside himself. "How can this be?" Joe asked. "I thought the hat was ruined and smashed flat as a pancake."

"It was," the hatmaker answered. "We fixed it. Come pick it up."

As it turned out, Delores had given the hatmaker the restaurant manager's name and number. Between the restaurant's manager and the large man who had been in the store, they had made arrangements to have a new one made. It looked exactly like the first one, except it wasn't flat and didn't have tea stains.

Joe picked up his new hat the next day. He was pleased with the hat and glad to have another custom-made one. This time, Joe took it home and placed a plastic weather cover over it. The hat took its place on the shelf at the top of his closet. He would never wear it on another trip or an airplane. Joe only took the hat out to wear on special occasions.

After twenty-six years of marriage, Joe had only worn the hat twenty-six times. He wore that hat at every wedding anniversary that he and Delores celebrated but at no other time. When Joe and Delores' son graduated from college, Joe gave the hat to his son Jeromy as a graduation gift.

The following year, Joe, Delores, Jeromy, and his new wife attended the National Finals Rodeo in Las Vegas. While on a Grand Canyon excursion, the hat blew off of Jeromy's head in a gust of wind. The hat plummeted to the bottom of the canyon and into the river below. The hat was never seen again. Joe and Delores just looked at each other and smiled. Delores said, "Well at least no one sat on it or spilled a pitcher of tea in it." Both laughed, blew the hat a kiss, and left. Joe made himself a promise. He would never again buy a custom-made hat. Their son Jeromy was beside himself and apologetic all the way back to the hotel. Jeromy's wife offered to pay for the hat, but it was to no avail. Joe and Delores were perfectly happy the hat had belonged to Jeromy and not to Joe.

On Joe and Delores' thirtieth wedding anniversary, Jeromy and his wife presented Joe and Delores with custom-made hats—one for each of them. All four attended the National Finals Rodeo with fifty-dollar hats on their heads. Their custom-made hats had stayed home, safe and sound.

By the way, the restaurant that Joe and Delores eat steaks at now requires their guests to remove their hats and store them in a custom-made closet. Now their fifty-dollar hats take their place beside all the $1,000 custom-made hats without any problems. Want a new hat?

Baseball and Beech-Nut

WE WERE JUST TEENAGERS IN A SMALL SOUTHERN CITY. OUR days were filled with fishing, hunting, and stories from our relatives. Most of the stories were exaggerated, but we didn't care. The stories were funny and exciting. The big thing for country boys was learning how to hunt, fish, and chew tobacco. Now that last one was something else. It would be a long time before we would tell our stories to our parents. They would have been furious if we had told when we were kids.

We stayed out of trouble most of the time. There wasn't a drug scene in our school. Teenagers having a beer in the barn or chewing tobacco were the worst things that we did. If there were drugs in our school, we didn't know anything about them. Clay and I hadn't heard of marijuana, and we thought that a joint was one of those places people went to drink beer. That was how naive we were.

It was baseball season in our town. Little League players practiced their skills and played competitively with their classmates. It was a sight to see. Many people from town watched the game, whether they had kids playing on a team or not. It was just one of the things that people did in our town. The same thing happened during football season. Everyone turned out to support their hometown team. This was not a southern thing. It was pretty much a universal thing.

Many of the ranchers and farmers chewed tobacco. Their children tried it for a while and eventually gave it up. The time to give it up was when they were old enough to go out on a date. The girls didn't particularly care for it.

Early on, many of our classmates tried it. Those guys didn't die from it, so we thought we would try it too. The following Saturday, we went to the local convenience store and bought Red Man and Beech-Nut chewing tobacco package. It was cheap back then. A package cost about twenty-five cents. It wasn't too bad for a boy who earned money in the summer hauling hay, mowing grass, or doing whatever it took to earn a few dollars. All the major league baseball players chewed tobacco. We watched them on television spitting now and then. We wanted to be just like them on and off the field.

Clay and I were about fourteen years old that summer. The older high school boys were doing it, so we tried a chew or two. We had to remember that we were city boys and not the sons of farmers or ranchers. They had more experience at that sort of thing. City boys usually didn't chew tobacco.

Clay and I wanted to win a bet that we had made with two of our classmates. They bet us a dollar that we couldn't chew tobacco without getting sick. Clay and I had already been practicing, but we didn't tell our classmates. We had already bought a package of Beech-Nut chewing tobacco. We kept it hidden in Clay's garage for a while. Then it came to my house for safekeeping. We were on our second package of chewing tobacco when the bet was offered by our rancher classmates. We decided to spring the trap at the next baseball game.

It was a hot afternoon. When it got dark, things would cool off a bit. We had finished our game earlier that afternoon. Our classmates were on the opposing team. We met behind the stands to show them our package of Beech-Nut chewing tobacco. They agreed that it was the real deal.

Our classmates took a chew themselves and then said, "Let's see if you guys can do this." The bet was that we had to keep the tobacco in our mouths for at least ten minutes. Clay took the first one and then handed the package to me. I took some chewing tobacco out of the package and looked at Clay's watch. "OK," the rancher said, "it's ten minutes to seven. Let's see how long it takes you to get sick. Bet you guys won't last five minutes. The clock was ticking as we stood there under those bleachers watching each other spit tobacco. It was two minutes after seven when Clay looked at his watch. Our rancher classmates were beside themselves. They knew they had lost the bet. They forked over a dollar each. Clay spit out his tobacco, but I kept mine in.

We went around the bleachers and climbed about halfway up. We sat a little to the left of the middle and tried to be nonchalant. I was certainly concerned about where I was going to spit. The first time, I spit down to allow it to hit the ground under the bleachers. Our two rancher classmates were still under the bleachers. They were about five feet to the left of us. I was worried about hitting one of those guys. The wind was beginning to pick up. Now and then, the wind would gust. I tried to spit only after the wind had died down.

We sat there for ten or fifteen minutes watching the game. There was a local rancher on one side of us and a group of parents on the other. Clay got up and went under the bleachers to get another chew. He returned about three minutes later. We sat there, chewing and cautiously spitting under the bleachers. One of the players hit a home run, and everyone stood up and cheered.

When we sat down, Clay had to spit. He had a mouth full of tobacco juice. Clay looked down under the bleachers to see if anyone might be under there. He couldn't see our classmates, so he spit. We didn't think anything about it. I was looking around when I noticed the rancher and parents still sitting next to us.

I turned and whispered to Clay, "We need to go."

Clay whispered, "Why? What's going on?"

I pointed to the rancher's starched, white shirtsleeve. When Clay had spit the last time, the wind had caught it, and then it had hit the rancher's right sleeve. He had not noticed it at that point. We wanted to be as far away as we could when he did.

About the time we got up. Another player hit a home run. We got up with everyone else and cheered. As we cheered, we quickly exited the bleachers. We ran under the bleachers and spat out our tobacco. We took our dollar and bought a Coke to wash down the smell of the tobacco. Clay also gave his remaining package of Beech-Nut tobacco to our fellow bet-losing rancher classmates.

We didn't go back to the bleachers. We figured it was time to leave, so we walked home. We knew the rancher would discover the tobacco on his crisp, white shirt. We didn't want to be anywhere near him when he did. We looked back after we paid for our Cokes. Our classmates sat down in the same place where we had been sitting. They were chewing our Beech-Nut tobacco.

When we got to school the following Monday, those rancher classmates were furious. After they had sat down, the old rancher had discovered the wet tobacco spit on his sleeve. He had quickly looked at the two boys chewing tobacco next to him. Guess who got the blame for the tobacco mishap? It was not Clay or me. Our friends got the blame, and they were ready to collect from us.

Chocolate Candy Bars

IT WAS TIME FO ROUR SCHOOL TO CELEBRATE. ALL EYES WERE on our small-town girls' basketball team, which had just made it to the state championship playoffs. Everyone was excited that our school's team was going there, especially the high school students. The varsity team had worked so hard to accomplish this goal. The citizens of our community were very proud and supportive of the team's efforts to get the school in the playoffs.

The date was set for the big game, and preparations were under way for the team to travel to Austin and bring home the State Championship title to our town. This was an exciting time for the school, and every student was anticipating a victory for our fair city.

The school decided to take an extra bus to Austin for the game watchers. The University of Texas hosted the event on its campus. It was an event to remember, especially for the busload of attending students. Each student who planned to attend the playoff had to sign up for the trip in advance. Many students put their names on the list. Each was asked to bring his or her own food for the four-hour journey to the university's campus. At the signup, they were also advised to bring some money in case they wanted to purchase soft drinks or food during our journey.

Some students brought lunch pails while others brought a brown-bag lunch. Some lunches consisted of a sandwich, bag of chips, piece of fruit, and soft drink. One of the students loved candy so he brought a couple of candy bars and cans of soft drinks. Each student had his or her own taste. Some brought a lunch and money to buy more things to eat on the trip. The excitement of the trip was definitely in the air no matter what was brought in their lunch bags. It was a four-hour journey to the university. The game would probably take about two hours in all, including the warm-ups, the actual game, and finding our way back to the bus. Afterward, there was another four-hour journey back home. It would be a long day, to say the least.

Early that morning, the students met in front of the school gymnasium, and they were checked off the list. Each person took a seat on the bus in no particular order. It was first come, first seated.

When all the students were loaded on the bus, they went into the early morning sunrise toward their destination. Among the attendants on the bus were a principal, escorting adults, and a driver. Three people could drive the bus, so relief drivers were not an issue. The bus had taken off on time. Each student was excited to be on the trip. None of the students had ever seen a state basketball playoff game before, so excitement loomed all over the bus.

Students chatted all the way to our destination. Laughing and talking were commonplace on any school bus, but this was different. The team had made it to the playoffs, and students were happy for our school's team to be there.

When they arrived on campus, the bus parked in its designated place next to the other school buses. They were given instructions about where to sit in the gymnasium and what their conduct would be while on campus. They were also warned about the consequences of any mischievous behavior. They were to support their team at the state playoffs, and they would conduct themselves accordingly. This was the stern warning from the principal. They were also told about the location of the concession area and restrooms.

The students left the bus, and in usual fashion, they were escorted from the bus to the gymnasium without disruptions. They entered the gymnasium and took their seats on the appropriate side. It would be a while before the game began, so some students took that opportunity to go to the restroom and purchase a soft drink and snack in preparation for watching the game.

They sat in their places and then looked around to see how the gymnasium was organized. Much thought was given to those on the other side of the court. They were from a small town too and their school had provided transportation to the game as well. The bleachers were not filled to capacity, but there were a great number of attendees. Some were from the news media, and others were there to film the game. Some were filming parts of the game to use when the news aired, but other people from the schools filmed it to bring home so that the coaches and players could see their performances and make adjustments for future games.

The game began on time. The players and the coaches were introduced as fans cheered for their perspective teams and players. It was back and forth and neck and neck the entire game. It was a good game for both sides as each tried desperately to gain the upper hand of the point board. Fans from both sides watched and cheered intensely as the game went on. Everyone knew that the team that won the game would go home with shouts of victory. The loser would go home in silence and dismay, thinking of how this long day had just got even longer. The stress would be on the players.

The game was over, and our school would go home sad and silent. Comments were made about what a great game the team had played and how close the team had come to bringing home a championship. It was a sad day for the hometown boys and girls as they gathered around the principal and staff to congratulate our team for a game well played.

Back to the bus the students went in the same order that they had exited it, but they had much less enthusiasm. Even though their team had lost the game, they were glad that they had been there to see a state playoff game. The greatest excitement was just getting to travel to and from Austin. Some students had not traveled that far in their short lives, so the trip was definitely worth the effort, even though a victory had not been achieved. The adults thought that the team would be back the following year and that it would be victorious.

As the bus pulled out of the parking lot and proceeded toward the highway, the students were still excited to be there. The game didn't have the desired outcome, but it was a trip away from home, and that was a thrill. The bus entered the highway and proceeded south toward home. A couple of hours later, the bus stopped at a service station. The students got off the bus, browsed the shelves, and then went back to their seats for the continuation of the journey.

The weather was hot that day, and the bus had no air-conditioning. The students were used to it, and they had no complaints. The windows were opened when students wanted it, so there was air flowing through the bus. Even though air was flowing, the temperature was still high.

One of the students pulled out his snacks from his bag and found a couple of unopened chocolate candy bars. He opened one and gave the other to the student who was seated next to him. They were all melted and a mess when they were opened. They looked at those sad pieces of chocolate that were just going to waste. The student still had a bag of potato chips, so he wasn't going to put the candy bar back in his bag. They decided to toss them out. They looked at the open window. Now these two boys were at the rear of the bus, so they thought no one would see what they were doing. They carefully watched the adults who were seated at the front of the bus. When the opportunity arose, out the window those two candy bars went. They were rid of the evidence, and no one was to know any different. A couple of other students witnessed the event, but they were silent.

Fifteen minutes later, the bus driver pulled into a service station and convenience store for the last stop before arriving home. An automobile pulled in behind the bus. The car belonged to one of the adults who had chaperoned the event. As the students exited the bus, a female adult approached the principal and asked him to follow her to her car. They proceeded to the automobile and saw the splattered candy bars right in the middle of the windshield.

The woman was irate. Her husband was making a vain attempt to wipe the mess off, but he wasn't making any progress. The melted chocolate was sticking to everything. Each time he swiped it with his handkerchief, it just smeared. It was a mess to clean up.

When the students had tossed the candy bars out the window a few miles back, both had landed in the center of the windshield of the car behind the bus. That car was a mess. Chocolate was melted chocolate all over that windshield. As the car pulled up to the gas pumps, they asked the attendant for some water and rags to clean the mess off the windshield. It took two people about fifteen minutes to get all the chocolate off the windshield and the wiper blades.

As the students gazed at the cleaning attempts, laughter broke out among the students. Comments went through the crowd of students as they watched the two adults trying to get the mess off so that they could see to drive. They were asking one another who tossed the candy bars out the window. No one was taking responsibility for that one.

The principal quickly dismissed the event and ordered all the students back in the bus. As they took their seats, the questions began. "Who threw those candy bars out the window? Anyone know? I know that someone knows who did it, and I'm going to get to the bottom of this." His attempts to determine who had thrown the candy bars out the window were in vain. No one spoke up. Silence fell over the crowd of students as they stared at the principal with sealed lips. The principal left the bus saying, "I'm going to give you students a chance to think it over. I'll be back in a few minutes."

When the principal left the bus, one male and one female adult remained on the bus. They just looked at us. The male adult commented on the accuracy of the tossed candy bar. It looked like he was going to break out in laughter, but he stood there and didn't say anything else.

The principal returned to the bus and asked once more who had tossed the candy bars. Again, all students were silent. No one said a word. There were only the blank stares. After a few more minutes, the principal allowed the students to go to the bathrooms and purchase items for the final leg of the trip. The bus left the convenience store about fifteen minutes later.

The bus arrived home that evening as the students jubilantly laughed about the candy bar incident. As all the students went their ways, the principal looked at them in disgust. He looked each student in the eye as he or she stepped off the bus.

Some of the students still chuckled and hung around as they waited for their rides home. The adults gathered in front of the bus. They looked at one another. Brief laughter broke out after one of the adults said, "Can you just see the look on Jim's and Margret's faces when those chocolate candy bars hit their windshield. There is no telling what was going through their minds as they attempted to wipe that mess off the windshield while the car sat on the side of the road." More laughter broke out, and then they were silent as they realized that some of the students were watching.

It was funny, unless of course, you had been the owner of the car. After seeing both of those melted, somewhat-liquefied chocolate candy bars hitting that windshield, it would have seemed like they had taken aim and tossed them out the window. It was food for thought.

Roy E. Staggs

Kline's Car

KLINE HAD THE FASTEST CAR IN OUR TOWN. FROM ALL AROUND the suburbs, people came to challenge the speed of his Chevelle. He was always victorious, and as far as I knew, he never lost a race unless it was when he had first started racing. He was a safe driver, and he always watched out for other people when he raced. He would never race on a city street. He always went outside the city to race someone. There was a remote place on the highway that was level and straight for about four miles.

Kline would not race his car against anyone for money, at least as far as anyone knew. One night, he was feeling confident about his car and his driving skills. Kline bet his vehicle against the other guy's car that he would win. It wasn't even close. Kline beat him by two car lengths.

Some of the high school students were there that night, watching and hoping that Kline would be victorious. Kline said, "There is no need to be concerned. I've got this guy in my pocket already. Watch his demeanor. He is already scared before the race starts. The time to be scared is after the race is over. That's when you know if you won or lost." Kline ended up with another car to add to his selling collection.

The guy came by the next morning to deliver his car with the title already signed. No one could believe that the guy had held up his end of the bet, but there it was. Kline's dad was not too happy about him betting on races that way. Kline's dad said that he should bet a lunch or something like that. They became mechanic friends. Kline eventually sold the guy's car back to him for half of what it was worth. Kline did some work on it before he sold it back to him. All of Kline's friends figured that he didn't want to take advantage of the man. He had a kind heart but also a willingness to succeed, especially at racing.

Kline had started his fast-car frenzy when he was in high school. In about his sophomore year, he began to drive. He was fascinated with races that were on television. He even went to the dirt tracks and the speedways to watch other drivers. He drove a couple of old cars that his dad had fixed up in the shop. He allowed Kline to put in the work to help pay for the car's parts.

The car was an old 1954 Chevrolet that his dad had taken in on trade. It was a heavy car but in pretty good shape for being that old. Those fifties' model cars were made of steel and were well-built automobiles. It had a six-cylinder engine and all the factory features, but Kline wasn't about to leave it that way. He began that summer by replacing the engine with one that had more horsepower. Kline always said that it was horsepower versus the weight of the automobile that made the difference.

Then Kline painted the car a different color—one with a metallic paint. Then he added mag wheels and wide tires, installed a lift kit, and raised its back. He also flared the fenders to accommodate the wide tires so that they wouldn't rub. It looked pretty good to all the high school kids. But Kline gave the impression that he wasn't all that satisfied with the car.

His fellow students saw it for the first time when he brought it to school one Monday morning. Most thought it was a fine-looking automobile. The adults thought that he had completely lost his mind. Most liked the factory look, but the high-school-aged kids wanted something different, and Kline wasn't going to disappoint. The next car Kline fixed up was a 1957 Chevy, two-door hardtop, and it looked great. It was green and white—the factory paint was still on it. I thought he would change the color a bit, but he just left it the way that it was. I guess he wanted the factory look for this one. He changed the engine from a six-cylinder to a V-8 and worked on the front end and interior. The car was fast all right, but there were faster ones in the area. Kline wanted to be the fastest by the time he was a senior in high school.

That '57 Chevy was just the start of his quest to build a fast automobile. Most of the students thought he had experimented on the first two or three cars that he had owned to see what he could do. Kline tested the applications of engines versus automobiles. He kept that '57 Chevy until the end of the school year.

The other high school kids began buying those older cars and changing them so that they had that hot-rod look. Many kids invested all the money they could earn to have a nice car. That was the trend in those days and even in the preceding years. Some people are still doing it in this day and time. Everyone loved those 1960s automobiles. They were well built and easily modified.

Kline liked those old cars. They could hold a larger engine without significant changes to the chassis. It was the thing to do. His next car would be the one that everyone remembered the most. He worked all that summer after graduation and bought a 1966 Chevrolet Chevelle. It was a nice car, even without any changes.

This car was Kline's pride and joy and the talk of the town. Even the cops admired his car and wanted one for a police vehicle. The city didn't buy them one. Every time they saw it, they stopped and asked him about the latest improvements that he had completed. All the students saw him at Dairy Queen and huddled around the car to admire his achievement.

That Chevelle was stocked just like it had come off the showroom floor. When Kline had bought it, it was already six years old, and it had about seventy thousand miles on the odometer. It still had factory-installed components. Kline had his work cut out for him. The age and miles on the car didn't seem to bother Kline. He knew because of his mechanical abilities that the vehicle was in good condition.

The young people couldn't wait to see what Kline would do to this newer model of car that he now owned. Would he strip it and start all over, or would he modify what was there? Would he paint it a different color and change the interior? Everyone was in suspense while waiting for his car to surface into the public's view.

Kline spent the entire summer working on that Chevelle. Kline's dad owned an auto-repair shop, so he had an advantage that most kids didn't have. His dad's shop had all the equipment most automobile-repair garages had. It had lifts, three covered garage bays, a covered area outside, and many tools and wrenches. The advantage that most didn't have in high school was air-powered tools. Those made it easier and faster to take things apart and reassemble them. By the time Kline was eighteen, he could take a car apart and reassemble it. Kline could also rebuild almost any component of an automobile.

His father was an excellent mechanic. Kline had a good teacher and had a natural ability to repair automobiles.

Everyone thought Kline would keep his automobile modification a secret until he was ready to unveil the finished product.

Much to everyone's surprise, as he would complete a specific project, he would come to Dairy Queen and show it off. Each time Kline brought it to Dairy Queen, there was a new improvement to the car. Some modifications were small, but with some modifications, even the unskilled car enthusiasts could see what he had done.

On occasion, the students who lived on his street went to his house and looked his car over. Kline explained what he had done. As each modification or addition was complete, Kline explained the why and the how. As time went on, everyone could see the gradual changes that he had made. He did an excellent job on each one. He must have spent thousands of dollars on that car. That wasn't too shabby for a hometown boy who had learned mechanics in his fathers' garage.

The summer after high school graduation, Kline was already working full-time in his dad's mechanic shop. Some kids brought their old cars by the shop from time to time. They had Kline look at the cars and tell them what was wrong with them. If it was something serious, they would leave it with Kline. His dad allowed them to pay the bill over time. Most couldn't afford mechanics to work on their cars, so Kline was kind enough to give them advice on how to repair the problem.

There were things Kline did to his car that he kept a secret. He didn't want his fast-car secrets to get to the competition. He shared general things but not everything he knew or did to the car. Everyone agreed that the car looked good and that it was going to become the fastest thing around our town. There was one thing that he did share about the engine. He was able to put over four hundred horsepower in a Chevy 396-cubic-inch engine. Most of the high school kids didn't understand all that was involved in engine horsepower mechanics, and most didn't want to know. The only reason that they talked about it was to brag on Kline's car. Those automobiles didn't have computers that could change the horsepower in an engine like they do today.

Kline's car had a large dome in the center of the hood. Under that dome, there were four two-barrel carburetors on a four hundred horsepower engine. This engine was certainly not fuel efficient when Kline put his foot heavily on the accelerator. The car averaged about eight miles per gallon of gasoline. Kline's vehicle was not a fuel-efficient automobile. In the 1970s, gasoline was less than a dollar a gallon. Kline wasn't interested in fuel efficiency but only speed. He wanted the fuel to burn correctly and give the engine maximum efficiency and the car maximum speed. Kline had to get that fuel ratio correct if he wanted to get the most out of every piston stroke.

When everyone saw the completed car for the first time, it was painted black with red and yellow flames down each side and across the hood and trunk. It was a masterpiece for everyone to see. When Kline opened the hood, mouths dropped, and eyes light up. Most kids probably didn't know what they were looking at, but everyone wanted to ride in that car.

A guy named Rick who lived down the street from Kline had fixed up an old 1949 Chevy pickup. It was an excellent-looking automobile, although it wasn't for racing. Kline helped him do some of the work on his pickup and gave him advice on what to do to the interior. Most of Kline's advice was regarding what engine to put in the car and how to strengthen the front end and other components. He installed rolled and pleated seat covers with extra padding.

There was no divide in the seat—pickups had bench seats back then, as did most automobiles. He also installed a glue-down carpet on the floorboards and behind the seat. He even put that glue-down carpet on the inside of the doors. They installed carpet behind the seat to help eliminate the echo effect that occurred when the stereo was playing. He went a step further with the carpet and put screws in it to hold it down along the edges.

Rick's dad found one of those small steering wheels that would look good to replace the huge one that came from the factory. The next thing that they installed was a foot emblem for the accelerator pedal. Rick's dad thought that he had lost his mind when he made all those improvements on an old pickup. The parents in those times were used to factory built cars. Modifying a perfectly good automobile must have been a sight for Kline's parents and their friends.

Doing all of this wasn't enough. More changes were needed to help its appearance and performance. Rick took Kline's advice except regarding one. This pickup was not going to be for racing. Rick replaced the engine with a V-8, but it was an all-factory engine with stock horsepower. Duel exhaust kept the engine noise low. Rick's dad didn't like loud automobiles, so he helped Rick with the exhaust to keep it quiet. There was one thing Rick did before installing the engine. He installed power steering and power disk brakes. That was unheard of back in the day. Rick's dad thought he needed to see a psychiatrist at this point.

Rick spent over a $1,000 on the front end and brakes. The best stereo speakers went behind the seat and under the dash, and a tape deck was added to the AM/FM radio. That sound system was just incredible. The point wasn't to have loud music. It was to have sound like you heard in a movie theater.

Rick added chrome wheels and wide tires with raised letters. Dallas had plenty of paint shops, so he had it painted candy-apple red. Since the interior was black, this looked great. Rick had a total of $6,000 invested in that vehicle. Rick was sure that his dad thought he wasn't spending his money properly, but it was his money, and fixing up a truck was better than some of the things the kids were doing. Rick's pickup was in no way associated with Kline's fast-car speed, but it was just for looks. Kline even helped with the design and installations. Rick was grateful.

Dairy Queen and some of the storefronts on the main drag seemed to be the places to be on weekends. Everyone would go in and buy a Coke or something to eat so that the manager would let them hang out in the parking lot. The manager said that as long as the kids didn't block the parking lot for the other paying customers, it was okay. Hanging out with our fixed-up cars and trucks was the thing to do then. Everyone looked forward to seeing what Kline had done next to his vehicle. Everyone thought that he was the man.

Getting a date was no problem for anyone who owned one of those types of vehicles. Rick and Kline didn't have any problems there. They weren't the best-looking guys in town, but they had jobs and cars, which were more than most had. Sometimes we would double date, and that enabled us to sit close to our dates. The girls quickly caught on to that and declined a double date in Rick's truck. In his senior year, he got a steady girlfriend. They cruised every Friday and Saturday night and had a blast.

One night, Kline was at Dairy Queen with his shiny car. He had just washed and waxed it. That car did look good. Guys and girls were gathered all around Kline's car, talking about the latest race that he had been in and bragging about it. One of them asked Kline what the top speed he had ever driven was. His answer amazed everyone. He said he that had been gone 140 miles an hour. Wow! Now that was fast. Like Rick's old truck, most students' vehicles were for looks, comfort, and anything that would attract attention. Kline had built his car for racing, and he did race it on the track sometimes too.

Many of the students went to watch Kline run his car. There was a picture of Kline's car with the front end off the ground as he took off from the starting line. That picture hung on the wall in his dad's office. Kline mostly raced his vehicle on the highways and short straightaways, but he was always aware of his surroundings.

Everyone knew Kline's dad was proud of his son but concerned for his safety. Kline never had an accident while he was racing. The following Saturday night at about two in the morning, Kline and Rick went for a ride. When Kline let off the accelerator, the speedometer registered 135 miles an hour on a straight stretch of highway near our town. Everyone was impressed to hear that. Rick said that he had been scared to death as he had watched the telephone poles passing by like they were a picket fence.

The next morning, Rick picked up his girlfriend and drove to the church. He told her about the run that he had had with Kline. She exploded. She said, "What if a tire blew out? What were you thinking? I don't want you to ride in his car again. I don't want to go to your funeral." Rick said that she started to cry when they parked at church. She was very upset about the incident. That was the end of Rick's riding with Kline or anyone who was going that fast. The next day shortly after the bell rang, ending that day's classes, the students flooded out to the school's parking lot. If one was not careful, one could be trampled by the kids who were leaving the school's grounds or run over in the parking lot.

Rick decided to go to Dairy Queen for a Coke and perhaps a snack. On the way, Rick saw that Kline doing the same. Kline had already graduated after the previous semester, but he still hung out with the students and his friends on the weekends when he wasn't working. After Rick went through the drive-through, he backed into a parking space. Kline parked next to Rick.

Rick and Kline had known each other since grade school. They lived on the same street, three houses apart. With the windows down, they chatted while they drank their soft drinks in the parking lot. Kline's girlfriend was with him. Rick's girlfriend knew her from school, even though she was a year or so older. Rick had grown up in that town, but he didn't know her. That didn't matter at the time. Rick had seen Kline with other girls before, but Rick's girlfriend said they were an item now.

Rick looked at her and said, "You mean like us?"

She laughed and said, "Of course, silly. They may even get married someday just like us."

Rick looked at her and said, "You don't say?"

After they had finished their soft drinks, they left Dairy Queen. Kline and his girlfriend were still there when Rick pulled out of the parking lot. He took his girlfriend home and then went home as well and changed out of his school clothes. Rick's brothers got a ride home with one of their friends and wanted him to take them to another friend's house to play basketball. Rick needed to pick up a new sports jacket at Steins, which his mom had bought for his upcoming school pictures. Rick called his girlfriend and asked if she wanted to ride over with him.

She needed to see the jacket. It was a chick thing. Rick took his brothers to their friend's house, picked up his girlfriend, and went to Steins. By the way, her name was Ellen.

When they turned onto the main drag, they noticed flashing lights a ways down the street. One lane on each side was blocked off, so they decided to see what was going on. There had been an accident of some kind between two cars, which were in the street. There were two police cars, a fire truck, and an ambulance. When they got closer, Rick saw that it was Kline's car and a Cadillac Fleetwood. There was no mistake about Kline's car. It could be spotted a mile away because there was none like it in the town.

They stopped, ran over to where Kline and his girlfriend were standing, and asked if everyone was okay. Kline replied in a soft voice, "Yes, we are OK. My car is the only thing broken."

Rick looked at Ellen and said, "He just washed that thing yesterday too and now look at it."

Kline was almost in tears, and his girlfriend was still shaking from the accident. Ellen hugged her and stayed close by her in case she fainted. One of the firefighters lived on Rick's street, so he asked him if everyone was okay. He said there were no injuries.

Kline and Rick walked over and took a closer look at his car. When they squatted down, they could see under the car. They saw that the frame of Kline's car was damaged beyond repair. The Cadillac had struck Kline's car right behind the driver's door. They were glad that the impact hadn't happened forward a couple of feet. A bent frame back then meant fatality for his fast car. There was no fixing it at this point. Kline would have to start all over again with another vehicle.

Some lady from out of town had been driving down the street at about thirty-five miles per hour. She had failed to see the stop sign. She hit Kline's car broadside. A Cadillac Fleetwood is a heavy automobile. It is like a Sherman tank and made of steel instead of fiberglass.

The wrecked cars were towed away from the scene of the accident. The bright side of the accident was that no one was injured. Rick had been in that car on the previous night going a 135 miles an hour. It was now totaled by a Cadillac going thirty-five miles an hour on a city street. Although it was unfortunate for the cars, everyone was glad that no one was hurt. Everyone walked away except the vehicles.

Rick kept his truck through college but sold it when he and Ellen got married. Kline didn't build another fast car for a few years. When he and Brenda married, all of that was behind him. The same was true for Rick. When their twenty-fifth class reunion came, Kline and Rick showed up in the same type of automobiles that they had driven in high school. The exception was that neither of the cars was a racing automobile. They were just stock engines with no loud pipes or anything like that. They just wanted to remember and drive their vehicles around town a couple of times a week to show them off.

One day, Rick commented that he wished his computer was as fast as Kline's car was in those days. He also said that he hoped they looked as good as his 1949 Chevy pickup. All things change with time, but they still say that boys never grow up; their toys just get more expensive. Rick and Kline's wives can attest to that for sure.

Rick, Kline, and some of the boys get together once a month to have breakfast or lunch together. They sit around and remember those days of fast cars and hanging out at Dairy Queen. All of them went on to recreate the cars that they had driven in high school.

They show up in those cars when they meet. All the people in the restaurant stop and gaze at the vintage automobiles and remember their days in high school as well. Most of the boys and girls from high school keep in touch. Once a year, as many of them as possible go on a cruise. It's like a reunion to them. They have a blast from the past. It's good to remember the past, but we must not dwell in it. We must live in the present, and on occasion, we go back and visit.

Never forget the past, as it will help you deal with the present. The past is our history. We can't forget the past because we don't want to repeat the mistakes that we made back then. God bless you.

A Faithful Encounter

EATING AT A LOCAL RESTAURANT WAS A REGULAR FRIDAY evening and Sunday after-church ordeal for me. I guess people kind of get in a rut after so many years, and it's hard to change those old habits established later in life. We get complacent and want things our way. It's not that we are out to change the world with our complacent habits. We like things to be our way, and we would like nothing more than for them to stay the same.

Things seem to change overnight—technology, computers, and so on. It appears that nothing ever stays the same for more than a month or so. Suddenly, it's upgraded and updated to a newer model, and everything you learned about the old one is gone. Learning a new program is an employee's only option. An updated version of the old program now exists. The only thing that remains constant is change itself.

There is one thing in this world that never changes: God. The Lord sets an event in place. It is a five-minute encounter that alters the lives of those who witness the outcome. I know that it did for me. I had found a restaurant that was always the same every time I went in there. The restaurant had attentive employees, good food, and excellent service. Tasty food and great service were the two main reasons for being in a restaurant on Fridays and Sundays. I got tired of cooking for myself. It wasn't that my food was all that bad, but I wanted to splurge. After all, I felt like I had earned it after all those years.

When I walked through the door, the staff already knew where I wanted to sit in the restaurant. Because I knew the servers, they, depending on the day of the week and time of day, knew what I usually wanted to eat. The sad thing is that I never liked being that predictable. The restaurant was a nice place to be after church to enjoy a good meal and sometimes sit and visit with friends I'd known for a few years. Other church members of different denominations also had the same idea.

The place had just replaced the carpet and re-covered its chairs and booth seats. They had redecorated the place to get a new look for itself. The décor was like a scene out of a movie that was set in the Deep South. It had good ole home cooking and friendly, courteous, and prompt service.

The young waitresses and waiters wore black pants or skirts, black vests, and white shirts. Although it was Texas, the staff didn't wear hats while working. I'd bet a day's wages that when the boys were off duty, they had them in their vehicles. I had one in my truck also. I had one on my head most of the time when I walked through the door. I grew up in the south where we wore hats on our heads and boots on our feet and had a gun in our trucks.

All young men had been taught since childhood to give respect and be polite to all ladies no matter what age they were. It didn't matter if the lady was a wife, a girlfriend, fiancée, stranger, or just a friend. Furthermore, a gentleman tipped his hat to the ladies and usually took it off when he entered the premises. A lady in Texas didn't open her own door unless she was walking alone. A gentleman always held the door for a lady. People in the South had a language and standards of their own.

We said, "Ma'am," to the ladies and, "Sir," to the men. We addressed our elders with respect. Ladies were seated before gentlemen took their seat at the table. We gave thanks to God for our meals.

Everyone's heart was blessed in almost every conversation. When we went to work, we provided the employer with a full day's work. I was alone in life. I was finally able to afford to eat a meal out now and again. I splurged twice a week: once on Friday or on a date and the other on Sunday after church. The restaurant was busy that afternoon, and my usual seat in the middle was taken by a couple, which was enjoying their anniversary. I usually sat in a small booth, which was not available when I arrived. Much to my dismay, I was seated in the bar area in a larger booth. I objected to the seating, but the restaurant was crowded, so I didn't have many choices. The reason that I objected was simple. I had given up drinking many years earlier, and I didn't want to be near the bar. A table or booth was the same there as it was elsewhere, and the food would taste the same no matter where I was seated. I preferred a booth, and that's what I got.

I had skipped breakfast that morning. I had only had a cup of coffee at about seven o'clock. I was hungry and needed a substantial meal to satisfy it. I could have gone elsewhere, but I liked the place.

At the bar, there was a younger man who had the body of someone who had lived a hard life. He wore a sleeveless Harley-Davidson T-shirt. He was the large muscular type. He was about six feet, two inches, and he weighed about 250 pounds. He looked like he was strong enough to take a guy out with one punch. He had tattoos on his arms and spoke with a bold voice.

I watched him slamming shots as his flirtatious attitude became more intense toward the young and attractive waitress who was tending the bar. As each drink arrived, he placed a five, then a ten, and then a twenty dollar bill on the bar for the bartender. He was hoping that she would respond positively to his tips and flirts. I had the idea in my head that he had done it before. His timing with the tips was connected to her presence and perhaps the end of her shift.

After my food arrived, I slowly ate my delicious steak, which had come with a heavily buttered baked potato with cheese and a house salad with a double dose of ranch dressing on the side. This feast was not my meal every Sunday, but I was hungry, so I had splurged on a good T-bone steak with all the trimmings. I could afford it during this period of my life. I had gone for it without any guilt at all. While I was eating, I was thinking about a delicious dessert to follow the meal. I had ordered a large glass of iced tea, which was lightly sweetened.

Steadily, the guy at the bar continued his pace toward the waitress for almost an hour as I finished my plate of food and a small piece of apple pie covered with ice cream. The meal was one befitting a king, and I enjoyed every bite. I can still taste my mom's apple pies and my grandmother's German chocolate cake, rainwater tea, and coffee served in a metal glass. This dessert wasn't it, but it was close. I'll tell you the truth. I missed those Sunday dinners with Grandma, Grandpa, and all those who gathered around the table for our feasts.

The task after dinner had always been to clear the table, put away the excess food, and wash the dishes. Then the adults would take a short nap.

I was well satisfied with my meal and iced tea. I needed to recover for a bit, so I sat there watching the overbearing man at the bar flirt with the waitress more intensely. He kept throwing money on the bar, and she kept taking his larger and larger amounts of money. I could see that she was getting tired of his advances and comments about going on a date with him and getting to see his new expensively decorated condo when he transported her there on his Harley-Davidson. I got the idea that she was getting upset.

I had seen her before in that area. She had beautiful features, and she could be flirtatious if she wanted to be. I remembered watching another guy doing the same thing, but her response had been much different. She liked the tips. She was usually very friendly, and she flirted back at the gentlemen, as long as they were kidding around.

But she was different today for some reason. She wasn't responding to this guy's flirts at all. I believe his attitude toward her along with his demanding tone and language would offend any woman. I could tell that he was the biker type by his tattoos, apparel, demeanor, and comments about trips on his bike. He had the look and tone of someone who had been around the block a time or two.

There was also something about him that appeared out of place. I got the idea that he was tired of all the road rage and running around the country on his infamous bike with his biker buddies. His language said one thing, but his eyes said another. Once, he turned and looked right at me and said, "Hi," with a nod of his head. I responded in the same manner.

He left for a few minutes to do what every person does after several drinks—to answer nature's call. When he returned, a new person was tending the bar: a man who was appropriately dressed as a bartender, had a smile on his face, and kindly asked if he needed another drink. The biker inquired about his beautiful young woman, in whom he had invested a couple of hundred dollars in tips.

"Oh, Mindi. Her shift ended, and she went home."

"Home," the man exclaimed. "I thought she was going to let me take her home." After he slammed his last drink, he stomped around for about thirty seconds and then headed for the door with some profane words coming out of his mouth. He left the bar and headed toward the front door while shaking his head in disgust.

He exited the restaurant and looked around outside for the young well-dressed bartender. He looked the parking lot over, but it was to no avail. He stood in front of the restaurant on the sidewalk, cursing himself and the young lady that he had invested a fair bit of time and money in. He had been hoping for a different kind of afternoon than she had been. Obviously, he wasn't happy about it at all.

I paid the bill, which had been left by my attractive waitress, and added a generous tip with no anticipation of a date. She was young enough to be my daughter. The waitress thanked me kindly, and we both went our separate ways, her to the next table of customers and me out the front door for my short journey home. I was going home to watch television and unwind from a busy week. My server went about her shift with a smile. She had seen what was going on at the bar too.

I walked toward the door with a smile. I was thinking about the guy at the bar who so wanted to take the waitress home. I laughed under my breath but not so that anyone could tell. I had seen this scenario play out before at other places where I had eaten. I saw guys treat female bartenders with disrespect at a bar or two when I was a drinking man many years ago. I didn't like that situation then and still don't like it to this day.

As I slowly walked out of the front door and toward my vehicle, the Harley-Davison man approached me with anger in his eyes. He poked his finger at my chest and exclaimed, "You thought it was funny how that waitress took me for a couple of hundred dollars."

I answered by saying that I had seen his actions and her actions as well. I asked the magic question, "Did you think she was going home with you?"

He promptly answered, "That's right. I bought and paid for that."

My answer was just as swift. "Never happen, sir."

He grabbed my shirt in a bunch and said, "I am going to kick you all over this parking lot." Actually, his language was a bit more colorful, but I promised the Lord that I would do my best not to use those words again.

My answer was a well-thought-out, "Since violence is your intention, let me tell you a few things about myself before you make a move. Then if you don't agree, you can have the first swing."

He reluctantly agreed and then let go of my shirt. His words were intense when he said, "You're going to get the beating of your life, old man."

I untied and slid off my tie and took off my jacket, laying it across my left arm. Then I threw it on the hood of a parked car, which was to my left. I looked directly into that huge man's eyes. He was over six feet tall and built like a bodybuilder. He had huge muscles, tanned skin, massive arms, and hands that looked like a construction worker's hands. I thought I was looking at a grizzly bear.

Then I began to speak with my eyes focused on his. "First of all, I've got thirty years on you, young man, and on my worst day, I could take you out in less than a minute." As he drew back his right arm, I placed my hand up and said, "Let me finish, explain myself, and see if you agree. In 1979, I was selected for the navy's SEAL program.

When I was active, I could kill you in a hundred unusual ways, and a few of them are excruciatingly painful. When I was a sniper, I killed thirty-four enemy soldiers and many others in close combat. When someone put his hand on my shirt in my violent days, I would have broken his arm off and handed it to him.

"I have twelve medals for bravery and even earned the Medal of Honor while being deployed on foreign soil, my last combat assignment before retiring. I served my country by answering Uncle Sam's call to duty. I graduated third in my class from the naval academy. I was deployed to serve in combat tours by four presidents.

"I will give you fair warning here and now. If you swing at me, I will defend myself with everything my country taught me, which could be deadly force. Everything depends on you at this point. Now comes the decision. If you still want some of this older man, let's get it on, but I have one last warning, I play for keeps, and I promise, you will not survive this encounter without multiple injuries. But that's OK, sir.

I am also a medic, so I will keep you alive until the ambulance arrives. So make your move, boy. I'm tired of talking." I spread my feet apart and placed myself in a defensive position, ready for the angry man's response.

The big man stared at me for a minute or two and then blinked. I knew that I had him at that point. Then he began to apologize for his actions by saying, "I didn't want anyone to say that I whooped up on a tired old man. That would be like kicking a child's butt."

As he turned to walk away, I gave him one last piece of advice.

"Young man, take it slow next time and be a gentleman. Everyone, including female bartenders, appreciates a man with respect and manners."

He turned, looked at me, and said, "Was any of that story true?"

My reply was simple. "Do you need to know?"

He shrugged his shoulders and said, "Guess not."

I picked up my jacket from the hood of the car, walked toward him slowly so as not to provoke him, and asked him if he attended church. His reply was one that I understood deep inside me. "Well," he said, "not since I was a kid."

I invited him to attend my church, gave him my cell phone number, and asked him to call me if he wanted me to pick him up on Sunday and take him to church. We both turned at the same time and walked to our vehicles. He stopped at a very nice black four-door Ford F-150 pickup. And wouldn't you know it, mine, which was the same vehicle except in white, was parked next to his.

We talked for a few minutes, and he said that he needed advice. I invited him to my small apartment, and for reasons that only the Lord knew at that point, he accepted.

We talked for over an hour, and he finally broke down and said that his girlfriend had left him because of his drinking and flirting with other women. He told me that he had been in jail in California for assault and that he had run with a gang out there who had robbed people, committed various crimes of violence, and acted immorally.

He seemed to be troubled by all of that.

I could tell that when he had been at the bar, he had been afflicted with painful thoughts about something, but I just hadn't quite been able to put my finger on it. Well, it wasn't for me to know at that time or ever for that matter. Only the Lord could reach him, so I just patiently listened and drew understanding from my violent days of military service.

By the Lord's hand and with his words, I led that man to Christ right there on my couch. I watched the tears fall from that big man's face as we kneeled on the floor. He confessed the sins that he had committed in his life. His final question was, "Do you think God will forgive me for all those things?"

My answer was swift and sure, "Yes, he will, just as he has forgiven me for mine. You are not alone in this old cruel world. You see, I killed men in combat and carried a heavy burden for years until I laid all of it down at the Cross."

I learned many things about him that day like his name being Theodore but everyone calling him Bear. The name seemed to fit.
He left my apartment after a hearty handshake. He had a different walk as he went to his vehicle. He slowly backed out of the parking space and drove away with a big wave out the window of his truck.

Bear faded into the crowd of vehicles on the heavily traveled street. I thought about what had just happened and suddenly realized that the Lord had set that whole event up. I believe that God intended for us to meet. A crowd of people had descended on the restaurant that day. My usual seating area was full. It was a chance encounter that took on a whole new meaning and chapter in my life and his.

I have always been told that God never closes one door without opening another. We must wait in close prayer and patient faith while the other door opens. We sometimes can't see the forest for the trees, so we get impatient and unruly. We think that God isn't listening. I want to assure you that God is listening, watching, and waiting.

As far as that navy SEAL story, I told the young man that we should leave it alone for the time being. I think that I was OK doing so because I avoided a confrontation, and to me, it was the whole point of the exercise. Avoiding violence saved his life and perhaps mine. The entire time the event was unfolding, I was squeezing in prayer between sentences and thoughts to ask the Lord to help me avoid violence one more time.

I had given up violence long ago and promised the Lord that I would avoid it, but I would not run from it. I never have in the past, and I will not, even today, run from it. I faced it just like I had in the old days. I promised the Lord that I would never take a human life again as I had in my military days. So far, I have abided by that promise. On that day, I wasn't sure that I could. I was relying on the Lord to weaken that man's heart so that I wouldn't have to defend my honor. I know myself better than anyone does, with one exception. The Lord knows more about me because he knows my past, present, and future. I only know my past and present. God sure blessed both of us that day.

I assure you that the Lord knows what he is doing, even though we don't realize it most of the time because we get so wrapped up in our lives. We are so busy with day-to-day things that we sometimes forget to stop in the middle of the day and say a prayer. As for the situation on that day, I knew that my soul was secure in the Lord, and I wasn't afraid to do what the Lord called on me to do: to be a good soldier for him and a good witness.

I think back on that situation every time I see Bear in church. He sits right behind me—the fourth row from the front and just to the right of center. He is not ashamed, and he always says, "The Lord and I have your back, brother," and I believe every word of it.

We became close friends and went on many visitations for the church in some not-so-popular neighborhoods and apartment complexes. I was glad that the husky giant of a man was on the Lord's side. We were never intimidated by anyone while on those visits. On occasion, we would meet one of his past acquaintances and even an old girlfriend of his. They were all amazed at his newfound life, and some followed in his path of serving the Lord.

Others cursed him when they found out how he had changed. Bear never flinched. He just kept on believing that someday, they would meet someone who could help them. For some of them, it was too late because they had already met their final destination.

Bear worked hard in that church for several years. He could do almost any construction project. But you know that the Lord has plans for all of us and knows when it is time for us to leave everything behind and move on to the next adventure.

Bear met with the youth director to see if he could help guide the young people on the correct path in life by sharing his experiences. His colossal size could be intimidating, but young people just loved him. He spent the next year working with high school and college students to help them see that a life with alcohol and drugs was for those who didn't love themselves, their friends, or the Lord. Although he was a bear of a man, he had a gentle side that motivated people.

When he talked in a low tone, it was as if the sound got inside a person. When he spoke in his usual voice, he could intimidate the most seasoned law-enforcement officer. I mention this because he also worked with troubled teens that the police were handling. He wasn't always successful, but I know that with the Lord's guidance, Bear brought many of them around to good living. I had such respect for him, and I was very glad that he was my brother in Christ. I would have hated to be a law-enforcement officer and try to put the cuffs on him, mostly when he was upset. No, sir, that was not for me.

Bear and I attended the same church for about four years. We often reminisced about our experience at the restaurant. That faithful encounter will forever be etched in my mind. We talked about how that led to a beautiful friendship. That encounter changed our way of life. We went on two missions' trips with the same group and even to youth camp as supervising adults. He had fun playing games with the teenagers and teaching a class or two. We had a blast and helped bring those in need of a closer relationship to Christ.

It was time for Bear to move on, and only the Lord knew when and where to guide him. We gathered at the church on a Saturday afternoon. Everyone showed up—even the older generation—to support the efforts. I sat on the third row and a little right of center. It was the same place that I had sat for so many of the sermons. The pastor delivered the message with inspiring eloquence. I sat there with joyful yet sad tears and listened to his eulogy.

Then it was my turn at the podium to speak the words that I had written a couple of days before that. I had an idea of what I was going to say. I just didn't want to lose control of my faculties. When I arose from my seat, I felt a helping hand on my shoulder. I was steady, calm, and ready to deliver a short message. Bear had said something to me one night that had almost floored me. "If I die tomorrow, what will you say at my funeral?"

"What are you saying? You're going to outlive me, so what are you going to say at mine?"

He had just laughed, and I had begun to say things about him that I respected and loved. His colossal size could be intimidating, but he was as gentle as a lamb. He was sure of himself, devoted, a servant of the Lord, and my brother in Christ.

Bear had looked at me with a tear in his eye and said, "Right on, brother. That's what I will say about you too, except I will leave out the navy SEAL thing." We both laughed about the restaurant encounter. I had already told him that was just a tall tale to get his attention directed somewhere else besides the violence he was ready to impose on me. I had practiced these words several times at home the night before. I could say them without tears falling down my cheeks.

When I got to the podium, I knew I wouldn't falter. I almost lost it a couple of times, but the Lord steered me through it. I could feel a presence around me, as if Bear were standing there with his hand on my shoulder. Sometimes I thought I heard him whispering, as if to steady me while I spoke. I related part of the story about how the Lord led us to one another and how he used situations like that to bring people to Christ. When the last speaker left the stage, there wasn't a dry eye in the house—mine included. I loved him as a brother, and I will miss him on this earth. But I know that I will see him again in our eternal home in heaven. God bless you.

Alfred's Week of Folly

ALFRED WOULD NOT HAVE BELIEVED WHAT THE WEEK WAS going to bestow on him as he sat in the police chief's office. The meeting began with some small talk. They asked how their families were doing. They discussed his career, his service record, and what his future plans were with the police department. The rumor was that the chief asked Alfred how long he had worked there, not counting tomorrow. Alfred replied quickly, "I have been here for about five years now Chief and still love my job sir?

They finally got around to his week of unfortunate events. The chief said, "I first thought, is he drinking or drugging? But all the tests came back negative?" The chief went on to say, "I can't understand how so many things can go wrong for one man in such a short time. I don't see anything in anyone's reports that indicate possible mental issues. Are you sure you are not having problems with any other officers or citizens or possibly at home?"

Alfred replied, "I don't understand it myself, Chief. No, there aren't any issues at home or anywhere else. The only stress I have is trying to explain the mishaps that occurred over the past week. It is just unbelievable. If anyone had told me these things would happen, I would have told them they were insane. We need to clean up this 'messterpiece.'"

The chief ordered the usual psychological testing and counseling to be on the safe side. Alfred complied with the chief's orders. That was the way things went for Alfred.

On Thursday, Alfred, a police officer for a medium-sized city in Anywhere, USA, had completed his evening shift's rotation. This city of about one hundred thousand citizens was no different than any other city that size. The local teenagers were up to their usual pranks and mischief. They had everyday speeding violations, domestic calls, and drunk drivers. There was usually a fatality accident and the infrequent murder. Burglaries, domestic situations, theft of property, and the usual speeders were all part of the things that Alfred dealt with. These were typical for a city that size or any city for that matter.

The police did have an ongoing investigation that was causing some issues. A few of the city's local businesses had been experiencing a rash of burglaries over the past month and a half. All patrol officers and detectives were on the lookout for the person or persons responsible for those incidents. The police department assured the public that they were working to find those responsible for the burglaries and bring them to justice. The public outcry was loud at this point, and it was about to heat up, but not because of the burglar. They would be concerned with the police department itself. A whole new image was about to be created.

Alfred had now completed nine consecutive days, and he was awaiting his three-day weekend with his family. He would rest and relax after those nine days of working burglary scenes and the rest of the mischief that occurred in the city. After his weekend rest, he would take the opportunity to prepare himself for the eleven-to-seven shift. This shift was eleven at night to seven the next morning. Hopefully, it would not be a full moon on his first night.

Alfred did not like the late-night shift because it was slow and boring. The night would creep by, and Alfred found it difficult to stay awake. His partners usually fell asleep on this shift. Alfred's wife was not happy with the shift either, but it was part of the rotation every patrol officer had to work. The good news was that some of the burglaries occurred on this shift, and Alfred might get lucky and catch the burglars. This would be a feather in his cap.

Alfred reported to work on Monday for his late-night shift. It was 10:30 p.m. when he pulled into the parking lot at the back of the police station. He parked in his usual space, which was not far from the back door. Alfred had not been issued a take-home vehicle. He used his personal vehicle to go to and from work. The back of the building had a security light and camera mounted on the wall. A streetlight shone on the parking lot as well.

Alfred exited his vehicle, opened the trunk, and retrieved his briefcase, shotgun, and the strapped bag containing his ammunition, backup firearm, and other equipment needed by on-duty officers. His hands were full. He wanted to get his gear inside and place it inside his locker. Alfred closed the trunk, slung the bag's strap over his shoulder, and put the shotgun on top of his right shoulder and pointed up toward the sky for safety. He picked up his briefcase and started walking toward the police station's back door.

Suddenly, the strap on his bag slipped off his shoulder. The bag quickly slid down his arm and hit the inside of his elbow. As his arm slammed downward, his finger hit the trigger on his shotgun. "Boom!" The shotgun fired one round of buckshot into the night sky. Alfred noticed that something fell, skidded by him, and narrowly missed his automobile.

Meanwhile, the police station fell silent and dark. Radios stopped working. Rooms all over the station went dark. The item that he had seen sliding by him was the power line to the police station. Alfred could hear the backup generator for the dispatch office start. Alfred just stood there watching in total shock. The live power cable sparked as it lay on the pavement. Two officers quickly exited the back door with guns and five-cell flashlights in hand.

One of them looked at Alfred and said, "You okay, Alfred?"

"Yes, I think so," Alfred replied, shaking.

"That sounded like gunfire. Was that you that made that noise?"

Alfred paused for about five seconds and then replied, "No, it was my shotgun that made that noise. It went off accidentally, and I guess it shot the power line in half."

Another officer laughingly replied, "Yes, sir, it sure did.

Congratulations, Barney—oh, I mean, Alfred. You hit it with one shot and without aiming." He turned to the other officer and said, "Go to the car and ask the patrol sergeant to come to the station." The officer made a beeline to his car and called the patrol sergeant. The officer then went inside the station and returned with two traffic cones. He placed the cones next to the downed power line for safety.

Alfred's pump shotgun had jammed when it had fired. He put his equipment on the ground and brought the shotgun off his shoulders.

Two officers watched as Alfred tried to rack the slide of the shotgun to eject the spent cartridge. Alfred pulled and pulled. Finally with one last tug, he racked the slide on his shotgun. When the shell ejected and the slide slammed shut, the gun fired again. That shot also contained buckshot. Another cable fell to the ground. There were no sparks this time.

As they looked up, they realized that the cable was the phone line for the entire police station. When that shot had been fired, the two officers had ducked. One officer stood up and grabbed the shotgun from Alfred's hand. He unloaded the gun through the magazine and then secured it.

"We are going to need this shotgun for evidence, Alfred. Pick up your equipment and put it here on this bench. Sit down for a minute and relax. We need to call the electric and phone companies to come and repair these cables."

One of the officers contacted the sheriff's department by radio and asked them to call the electric and phone companies and tell them to respond as soon as possible. When the phone system went down, it automatically transferred all calls to the sheriff's department. That was a good thing.

Two more officers, who had heard the gunshots, came to the station. After asking what had happened, all four began to laugh. Alfred could have crawled under his bench. How embarrassing it was. It was a good thing that no civilians were watching. Everyone in the downtown area must have heard those shots. They hoped the burglars heard them and went home in fear of their lives.

One officer commented, "Well at least no one can call and complain. We have no phone service."

The patrol sergeant arrived, just stood there, and looked at the mess that Alfred had created. He could not believe what had just happened. He thought everyone must have heard the shotgun blasts. He kept shaking his head in speechless thought. The Sergeant looked up, down, and then at Alfred. None of the officers could remember this ever happening before. I guess there is a first time for everything.

The Sergeant said, "OK, Alfred. Go inside and file your reports for the chief. I would not like to be in your shoes when the chief finds out about this."

The chief of police was called. He came and inspected the damage. He had the same thoughts that the patrol sergeant did. *How could this happen?* He hadn't seen such a thing like this happen in his entire twenty-five years on the force.

The electrical and telephone companies restored services to the police station. Alfred completed his report on the incident and went on patrol with a rookie partner. Even though the shift started with a loud bang, the rest of the shift was quiet and uneventful for the most part. Alfred kept saying throughout the shift, "I can't believe I shot those lines down. I can't explain it. How am I going to live that one down?" On the following night, his shift was typical—with one exception. When Alfred arrived for work, he put his equipment and gear into his patrol car. The rookie was a minute behind Alfred. When they inspected their vehicle, they noticed that the right rear tire was flat.

Now they had to change a flat tire without getting their uniforms dirty. Alfred and his rookie partner did not make a single arrest. They also didn't experience any significant events. They handled a few minor calls, and there were no adverse outcomes. This was a good thing for Alfred. No one knew if Alfred could take another power and phone line incident.

On the third day of their night shift, Alfred and his partner were ordered to patrol the city's downtown section when not answering calls. Some of the burglaries had occurred in this area of the city. The businesses had to be checked, front and back. After a few minor calls, they drove down an alley behind a row of storefronts in the downtown section. One business was a check-cashing office, one was a hardware store, and one was an electronics' business. There were other businesses in the shopping center, but none would be likely targets for burglars.

While in the alley, they noticed that a car was parked behind the hardware business. Suspecting a burglar, they pulled around in front without their headlights on. They stayed about a hundred feet back from the door in a dark part of the parking lot. Alfred placed the gear shift in the neutral position, left the car running, and set the parking brake. Although that not protocol, it sounded reasonable to the rookie officer. The rookie thought to himself, who was going to steal or vandalize a police car with two officers standing nearby? This had to be his reasonable assumption.

One walked to the left while the other walked to the right side of the hardware store. As they peered into the building, the rookie saw the car's reflection in the window and thought that Alfred was moving the car closer to the door. He continued scanning the inside of the building. As the rookie turned to see the reason that Alfred was moving the vehicle, he noticed Alfred standing on the other side of the hardware storefront. When Alfred turned, he saw the squad car barreling toward the store. Then he caught a glimpse of the rookie standing on the other end of the business. They watched in horror as the squad car plowed through the window and stopped just shy of the rear door of the car.

The rookie said, "I thought you saw something and were moving the car closer to the door." Neither of them had a better explanation.

Alfred approached the car as the rookie paused when he saw the disgusted look in Alfred's eyes. Alfred looked up and said, "Why is this happening to me? First, the power and phone lines and now this. In five years on the force, I have never had anything like this happen to me." About that time, the owner came speeding around the building and parked in front of it. As he jumped out of the car to approach Alfred and the rookie, two more police cars arrived on the scene. The owner had called the police station, thinking the burglars were making one final take of his store's items.

The patrol sergeant arrived on the scene and just stood there in disbelief. "Alfred, what in the world just happened here? Tell me that you let the rookie drive tonight and that he wrecked the car." There was no response from Alfred, other than looking down at the pavement. "Don't tell me that you drove that patrol car into this business. Please tell me the brakes failed."

"No," Alfred replied with a loud tone, "I sure didn't drive the car into that business. And no, the brakes didn't fail. And no, the rookie didn't drive either. I do not know what has been happening to me lately. Maybe I need a vacation."

The sergeant replied, "I don't know about a vacation, but you sure need something." The sergeant turned to the rookie and asked, "Did you see what happened here?"

The rookie said, "You should probably talk to Alfred about that."

The sergeant replied, "We're going to do just that and you as well.

Call for the crime unit to take pictures of this. The chief will not believe this without pictures."

The damaged building had to be secured to prevent vandalism.

The next day, the city paid a company to repair the damaged window and frame. It must have cost the taxpayers a lot of money to repair the damages to the hardware store.

Alfred's next shift went just like it should have—well, kind of. It was a busy shift, and this helped Alfred keep his mishaps off his mind. Alfred and the rookie officer went home on time. They had arrested a drunken man outside of a business. Evidently, he had been unable to drive home, so he decided to walk. It was a little cool that night, but the man didn't have a jacket on. Alfred thought that the liquor must be keeping him warm.

They made the arrest and located his car. It was legally parked, so they didn't have it towed. They were kind enough to notify the man's wife of the incident. They took the man to the county jail, and on arriving, the man hurled in the back seat of the car.

The rookie exclaimed, "Why anyone would put carpet in a police car I will never know. Rubber floor mats would be better."

They had a trustee at the jail come out and clean the inside of the car, but it smelled awful the rest of the night. Nothing could get that smell out of the car. It was unfortunate that the incident had occurred in the first three hours of their shift. Although the car was undamaged, it smelled awful for the next shift as well.

When he got home, he met his wife leaving for work. She looked at him and asked, "Did everything go okay on your shift? No incidents to report?"

Alfred replied with a sharp tongue, "Nothing other than a drunk hurling in my car. That car still smells bad. Go to work so I can get some sleep."

His wife left for work and Alfred went to sleep. Although this incident was something that occurred occasionally, the next shift would prove to be something for the record book.

Alfred and his rookie partner began their next shift at eleven o'clock that night. The car still had a slight smell, but this time, it smelled of all kinds of cologne, sprays, and who knew what. The odor was bearable, especially with the windows down. Alfred's partner brought some cologne and sprayed the car again. That helped enhance the smell even more.

They attended the shift briefing, held inspections, loaded the patrol car with the necessary equipment, and then drove off into the night.

Alfred had his usual brown bag full of snacks in the front seat. They patrolled awhile and answered two citizen calls. The last call that they worked on was a disturbance call where a drunken man tried to grab Alfred's gun in a scuffle. The man was arrested and taken into custody.

By this time, Alfred and the rookie were ready to take a break from the action. They proceeded to the nearest convenience store for a soft drink. On slow nights, the officers could take a break or two.

Alfred and the rookie loved Classic Coca-Cola in the can. They purchased one each and proceeded outside the shopping center to their car to enjoy their soft drinks and snacks.

They were not on official break, so they stayed in the car to listen to the radio for any calls that might be dispatched. After they parked, the two officers rolled the windows down, opened the brown bags of snacks, and began to eat. The first thing out of the sack was a package of beef jerky. This was one of Alfred's favorite snacks.

As Alfred and the rookie chewed on the jerky, they opened their canned Cokes simultaneously. The Cokes exploded in their faces and all over their uniforms and the car's front seat. Coke was even on the windshield and dashboard. Coke sprayed everywhere. It must have been a sight. They jumped out of the car, opened the trunk, took a water jug and two clean rags out, and began to clean Coke off their faces. They made an attempt to clean themselves and the inside of that car. That was all that could be said. It was a sticky mess to clean up.

I'll bet that the convenience store attendant is still laughing about shaking up those Cokes for his fellow public servants. I believe that he would love to have seen that Coke-spraying incident go down. They had just finished the cleanup when a call about a prowler came over the radio. They were only three blocks away from it, so they went, still covered in sticky Classic Coke.

The dispatcher still had the caller on the phone when they arrived, but she refused to come to the door until they caught the man who had been peeking through her windows and trying to break into her house. Both officers took defensive positions beside the shrubs that were in the front yard. Alfred went to the left side of the house, and the rookie went to the right. They planned to meet in the backyard. Each scoured the shrubs and bushes and checked all the windows on the sides of the house.

As the rookie opened the gate to the backyard, he heard Alfred let out a horrible scream. The rookie ran around the house, with his gun in one hand and his five-cell flashlight in the other. When he arrived at Alfred's location, he found him on the ground. A large Labrador retriever was pawing and licking Alfred's hands. The dog had smelled the Coke

91

and beef jerky on them. The dog had come up behind Alfred and licked him on the hand. It had scared him.

The rookie laughed and said, "Is this the prowler we were looking for?" Alfred didn't think it was so funny. They proceeded back to the car and contacted the dispatcher. Alfred wanted the elderly occupant advised that they had the prowler in custody. The dispatcher informed the occupant to come to the door and talk to the officers. When the occupant came outside, the dog ran up and began licking her and wagging its tail. The occupant was the dog's owner.

"Lucy," the owner said, "where have you been?" The gate had slammed shut, preventing the dog from entering through the dog door in the backyard. The officers determined that the dog must have been scratching at the door and windows as it had tried to get back into the house. The owner thought it was a prowler trying to get into the house. The rookie had thought that Alfred had had a heart attack, but he had only been frightened when the dog licked his hand and jumped up to greet him. Alfred assumed it had been the prowler trying to get his gun away from him like the drunk had an hour or so before that.

The dog-prowler report ended with the sergeant saying, "You seem kind of on edge tonight, Alfred. Are you sure you are okay?" Alfred was almost in tears because of all the things that had happened to him that week. They had only two shifts left on their rotation, and they couldn't be over too soon for Alfred and the rookie.

The last incident for Alfred occurred on the sixth day of his late-night shift rotation. The night had only been busy: two minor accidents, three citations written for speeding, and one DWI arrest.

After they cleared the jail, they began to patrol in a largely residential section with expensive houses. Burglars usually liked those neighborhoods. They were typically good scores for burglars.

Alfred had stopped at the first stop sign on the quiet residential street. A small sports car went speeding by them. Alfred engaged the warning lights and took off after the vehicle. The driver complied with the warning lights and pulled to the curb. As Alfred exited the car, his seat belt became entangled with his gun belt.

"Now, what's going on here? Get off there," he exclaimed to the seat belt. He freed himself and walked toward the parked car. The rookie approached the vehicle from the passenger side as Alfred arrived at the driver's door. They were both taking cautious approaches per protocol. Both thought this could be the burglary suspect.

Now Alfred was about six feet tall, and the sports car sat low to the ground. Alfred bent over to ask the driver for his license. He then asked if there was an emergency to justify the excessive speed in which the car was traveling.

The driver replied, "No, no emergency. I just got to listening to the radio and lost track of how fast I was going." How many times had they heard that answer?

When Alfred bent over, his gun fell out of his holster. Evidently, when the seat belt had become entangled with his gun belt, it had unsnapped the strap that held his weapon in the holster. Before Alfred began questioning the driver, he handed the driver's license to the rookie and asked him to check for warrants and wants. The driver noticed that the gun had fallen out, but Alfred had not. The driver called Alfred's attention to the fallen gun. Alfred quickly picked up the gun, holstered it, and thanked the driver. There were no warrants for the driver, and there was no merchandise in the car or the trunk. There were no citations issued, and the driver and officer went on their way.

Two months later, it was time for Alfred to demonstrate his proficiency with a firearm at the shooting range. Every police officer must demonstrate proficiency with his or her weapon. Eight other officers were at the firing range trying to qualify with their weapons.

Alfred's turn was next, and as he approached the shooting position, he un-holstered his weapon, checked it to make sure it was loaded to capacity, and then secured his weapon in his holster. The order came to un-holster their weapons and fire six rounds at the silhouette in front of each officer.

Alfred drew his weapon and pulled the trigger. Instead of discharging, Alfred's gun reported with a, "Click, click, click." Alfred rechecked his gun. There were bullets in the gun—six to be exact.

He raised the gun again and heard, "Click, click, click." Alfred went to his patrol car, retrieved his backup weapon, and returned to complete a successful qualification on the range.

The range master took Alfred's weapon and had it examined by the police's gunsmith. Upon inspection, the gunsmith determined that the problem was a broken firing pin. When Alfred had dropped his gun that night of the traffic stop, it had broken the firing pin. For two months, Alfred had been carrying a weapon that would not shoot. It was a good thing that he didn't need to use the weapon in the line of duty to protect a citizen or himself.

Alfred's week of working late nights ended on the seventh day of his rotation. The night was just incredible. There were no incidents that caused any problems with weapons, exploding Coke cans, dog-licking events, or store-owner complaints.

His rookie partner had only one incident on that shift. After exiting the patrol car, he ripped his pants when he bent over to pick up the gun after dropping it in the parking lot. Alfred advised him to have it checked on the following day so that the weapon would be in good working order.

After Alfred left the station to go home, he stopped at a convenience store to purchase oven-baked peanuts and a Coca-Cola. When he pulled into the driveway at his residence, he opened the door, exited, and walked to the end of the driveway to retrieve the newspaper. When he returned to the car's open door, he sat down in the seat, reached to pick up the bag of peanuts and his coke. When he grabbed the bag of peanuts, something crawled up his right arm, across the back of his shoulders, down his left arm, and then exited the car. As this was going on, he let out a bloodcurdling scream, which was much louder than the dog-licking event.

While he had been retrieving the paper, a squirrel had entered his car. It had been attempting to eat the peanuts. When Alfred had gotten back into the car, it had startled the squirrel. The squirrel had taken the only way out that it could.

Alfred's wife had already been at the door and had heard him scream. She had bolted through the door, thinking he was a would-be thief who was trying to steal his car. His wife had come to a sudden halt at the car when she had recognized Alfred sitting in the front seat.

She now stood there looking at her husband and laughing. As Alfred's wife had seen the squirrel exit the vehicle and climb the nearest tree. She squatted down in from of him, still laughing. His Coke was still in the drink holder unharmed. Alfred handed the coke to his wife, who promptly started to open it so that she could give her husband a drink. When she opened it, it exploded, spewing Classic Coke all over her, Alfred, and the front seat of his car. That was the only significant thing that happened to Alfred that day.

The events that took place in Alfred's profound night-shift were unfortunate. After shooting the power and phone line and disabling the entire police station for three hours, he had received a three-day suspension for the accidental discharge of a weapon, causing property damage. After the squad car had plowed through the hardware store's window, he had received two days off without pay.

The chief cited that the owner had been inside the store at the time of the incident. Alfred was charged with endangering a citizen, failing to secure his automobile, and damaging private property. Alfred's days off without pay would run concurrently, and they started on his next shift rotation. Sometimes it took time to get the paperwork through and reach a decision. When the shooting range incident had occurred, Alfred had been given a two-day suspension without pay.

He was charged with failure to keep his weapon properly maintained and endangering a citizen during a traffic stop. Alfred had not been disciplined for the squirrel incident because it had occurred while he had been off duty and it hadn't violated any police policies or procedures.

The following year Alfred was promoted to patrol sergeant, where he taught rookies proper ways of securing weapons and police vehicles. Two years later, Alfred received another promotion. He was promoted to deputy chief of police in his fair city. He could retire in a couple of years. The other officers hoped that he would. Alfred was awarded a citation for having fired his gun only twice in the line of duty during his twenty years of career service in law enforcement.

He would most likely become police chief when the current chief retired. By the way, the officers who witnessed Alfred's follies still called him Barney, that is, before he became deputy chief of police. Alfred no longer bought Classic Coke in a can. His wife refused to buy it for him, even though aluminum was selling at a high price at the salvage yard. She now purchased Classic Coke in plastic bottles.

As for the rookie, he was now the patrol sergeant. He developed a new policy for the patrol officers. There would be no soft drinks allowed in the patrol cars. He had learned something from Alfred after all. Secondly, he supervised a weapons' inspection at the start of every shift. He had had a spotless record since he had quit riding with Alfred. There was another improvement for the police department. When Alfred became deputy chief, the current chief of police made some changes of his own. When the city built a new city hall, the police department was moved into one end of the new building. The building consisted of modern improvements, such as a backup generator in case they lost power. Each employee also had an assigned parking space at the back of the building and away from the electrical and phone system. All electrical and phone lines were underground. No overhead wires went to the police station or city hall.

Alfred was once again credited with creating an improvement to the city's facilities: all the underground utilities. New police vehicles were now equipped so that the keys could be taken out of the ignition without turning off the engines. Alfred had seen that as a problem, especially when exiting the vehicle. A special consideration was given to this new feature. The keys couldn't be taken out of the ignition unless the gearshift was in the P (park) position. Alfred and the new patrol sergeant thought it was a great idea.

New officers also had their problems and situations to deal with. Their cars were equipped with GPS, which tracked their cars' movements, speeds, and locations, every minute of the day. The dispatcher could see where each vehicle was located when dispatching a call.

Modern technology solved many problems for most city workers, especially where the police department was concerned. The only thing technology could not solve was the human factor. The department called it the Alfred Syndrome.

Grandma's Chocolate Cake

THERE WAS NO DOUBT ABOUT IT. GRANDMA WAS AN excellent cook, as were her children. All of her grandchildren bragged about her chicken and dumplings, quail smothered in brown gravy, and her roasts. Other favorites were brisket, fish, homemade sausage, and venison. She could make any meat satisfy anyone's appetite.

Grandma always said that it was the way the meat was prepared that made the difference. Grandma could make any meat taste good. Other favorites were the fresh vegetables that she served at every meal except breakfast. Grandma and my mother fried, boiled, or baked those vegetables to perfection. Lunch and dinner had another delicacy: sweet rainwater tea served in a metal pitcher. Although these were excellent meals, her cakes and pies were the favorites of everyone seated at the table, especially her grandchildren.

The one that was favored the most was her made-from-scratch German chocolate cake. Now those cakes were loaded with mouthwatering, finger-licking flavor for the taste buds. Those cakes would make your mouth water just by looking at them. There must have been a million calories in one of her German Chocolate cakes, but we didn't care.

The grandkids thought they were huge, but depending on how many grandchildren were in attendance, there was never enough for seconds. Grandma would bake a pie too. Many times, there was homemade ice cream to put on top of those apple pies. Anyone would say that these meals were not for someone who was on a diet.

To house the cake and pie, grandma had a couple of those plastic cake covers. These were used mainly for the cakes to keep the fingers out of the icing. The big surprise was when the deserts were brought to the table and uncovered for the first time. There was no peeking allowed under those plastic covers. I remember Grandma slapping my hand when I tried to peek at what I suspected was the German chocolate cake. Grandma and Grandpa were of German descent, and they worked hard all their lives. They were farmers and made everything stretch as far as they could. Money was many times in short supply, but nature played a role in their food supply. They hunted, fished, grew a vegetable garden, and had an orchard full of fresh fruit. The fresh fruit came in handy when it was time to make peach preserves, cobbler, plum and grape jelly, pecan pies, and all those other heavenly desserts. Many times, her family would comment that if you left their house hungry, it was your own fault. Most of the farming and ranching families were in the same situation. Grandma always offered to prepare a meal when anyone visited.

Those weekend adventures to the farm were exciting for the grandchildren. They yielded good food and time to visit with uncles, aunts, and cousins. All the cousins remarked on how good those visits were and welcoming the family was on those visits. Each family contributed something to the event. Sometimes they brought their musical instruments. Each family would bring food to Sunday meals. Sometimes a family would bring meat that was to be frozen and served at another time. During hunting season, the family would bring whatever they caught that day.

The adults sat at the main table. The children sat at a smaller table or outside on the porch. The parents would dish out small portions to their children. No one went hungry at Grandma's table.

I always looked for the dessert. I wouldn't say that I liked some of the vegetables that were served, but I loved those pies and cakes. I remember turnip greens being served at some of the meals. To me, those were the worst. I always chose to sit outside so that I could throw my greens away without Mom or Dad seeing me. I would gag just looking at them. My parents always wanted me to eat at least one vegetable like squash, okra, or corn.

There were always black-eyed peas, shelled peas, green beans, tomatoes, fresh green onions still on the stalk, potatoes, carrots, and so much more during the summer. My grandparents canned or froze everything that they could for the winter. Grandma usually made gravy to serve with the meal. My plate always had potatoes smothered with gravy, corn on the cob, beans, a slice of meat, and of course, a glass of rainwater tea.

I didn't mind fried squash or fried okra. I liked corn on the cob. These three would take the place of the turnip greens. Sometimes grandma would boil the okra and squash. That's when I knew that I was not going to have a good visit. I might be able to choke down some squash but never okra. To me, boiled okra was no different than turnip greens. Boiled okra was slick and slimy. Yuck!

There was another delicacy served at our German grandparents' home. This delicacy was sauerkraut and sausage. I could eat the sausage, but the sauerkraut was a no-brainer to me. To this day, I'm still not too fond of the smell of boiled cabbage. Grandma said that sauerkraut was an acquired taste. Yes, she was correct, but it was a taste that I never acquired. It was not as bad as turnip greens or boiled okra, but it was close.

Many people ask why some children do not take after their parents when it comes to food. The grandparents here are my mother's parents. They were all raised as farmer's children. They worked hard and ate their fresh vegetables. My parents were hardworking people too, but money was also in short supply. We grew vegetables to help supplement the grocery bill. Later in life people often asked me why I didn't like many fresh garden vegetables when we were so poor and grew a garden to eat from. I just didn't have a taste for most of them, especially the green leafy ones when they were boiled and ready to eat. My parents and grandparents often said that wasting food was a sin. I could have given all those kinds of vegetables away if it were up to me. Most didn't waste anything in those days. I can't explain it.

Enjoying eating vegetables must not be a hereditary trait. It certainly wasn't for me. Now dessert was something that I did inherit from my family.

With many families of that day, if the children didn't eat their vegetables, they didn't get any dessert. I was usually the one without dessert. One of the things that I liked at Grandma's house was that everyone got dessert. It didn't matter if the grandchild left his or her vegetables on the plate. When a child misbehaved or threw a temper tantrum, then that child would be denied dessert. Denying dessert to a child was the worst punishment that one could receive in those days. No grandma's German chocolate cake was the ultimate punishment.

We usually spent one Sunday a month at our grandparents' house for lunch. One or two of my mother's siblings were usually in attendance. On this particular Sunday, my uncle and three of his children were there. Per grandpa's request, each had brought a contribution to the meal. We were ready to eat at about one o'clock that day. Grandma's table could seat about ten people if the children sat on the bench's side of the table. The adults took their places at the table. The food began its slow journey around.

There was no boiled squash or boiled okra on the table. To my joy, there were no turnip greens either. That day was going to be a good day for one child—me. I chose my usual beans, potatoes, gravy, and corn. I had my regular glass of sweet rainwater tea. I could see the look on my mother's face when she saw me smile, demonstrating my joy about there being no okra, turnip greens, or squash. She smiled back. The end of the meal would be a defining moment. We knew that we could have a slice of German chocolate cake or a piece of pie.

We thought that we were having the feast of a king at this point. The children would get a glass of milk and one slice of pie or cake.

Everyone knew what my choice would be. There were five cousins present. Three chose the cake, and two chose the apple pie. Each could have one scoop of homemade vanilla ice cream on top of the dessert.

The cake and pies were in the plastic containers on top of the deep freezer. My grandparents had a deep freezer for several years, and it was one of the larger versions. This freezer was large enough that many had a hard time reaching the bottom of it. I kept looking at the cake and pie containers. I wondered who would get the dessert down from the top of the freezer.

Some of the adults had left the table and gone outside. Grandma, my mother, and my aunt were clearing the table of dirty dishes. The five children were still sitting at the table talking and awaiting the dessert. My aunt poured each of us a glass of milk. She also set a dessert plate in front of each one of us.

Grandma called out to the children, "Someone get the pie and cake from the top of the freezer and get the ice cream out." My older cousin was strong enough to lift the freezer lid, so he got up to help. My older brother and I got up to get the pie and cake. Both of us reached for the cake at the same time. We debated for a second or two about who was going to carry it to the table. As we struggled back and forth, the plastic lid came off. All I remember hearing was,

"Splat." Grandma's German chocolate cake fell flat on the floor in utter ruins. As the cake fell, my brother turned, stumbled, and stepped in the center of that cake. It was a disaster of gigantic proportions.

We just stood there looking down at the floor and the beautiful cake. I looked at my brother's shoe, which had the remains of the delicious cake on it. We knew that we were in trouble. Not only would our feelings be hurt but also our backsides would probably be feeling the pain of a willow switch. We thought that the denial of the German chocolate cake was the worst of it all. The pain of the switch only lasted a few minutes. The memory of that cake would remain for a lifetime. This incident would especially be recalled by our cousins, who constantly reminded us from that day forward. I remember a cousin asking me years later, "When the last time you ate German chocolate cake off the floor?"

Grandma and my aunt came out of the kitchen at the same time. They saw us staring at the floor in utter disgust. They just stood there staring at the floor. Finally, Grandma said, "How did this happen?" My brother and I shrugged. I said, "I don't know. It just slipped out of our hands, I guess."

My older cousin gladly offered an explanation by saying, "They both grabbed the cake, and when they turned around, it slipped out of their hands. It looked like the top was not snapped on tight." Grandma said, "I guess I didn't snap the lid on when I set it down on the freezer." My brother and I didn't get any dessert that day. My mother stood there in embarrassment as she watched us clean up the mess. I knew for sure that we were going to be disciplined when we got home that afternoon. My brother and I were dreading the trip home.

We knew that my dad would lecture us the entire eighteen miles home. It was unusual for our dad not to say anything. When we were did something we were not supposed to do, there was always a lecture. Following that lecture, there was a lesson to be learned. If warranted, discipline followed. Much to our surprise, Dad didn't say a word. He just stood there watching us with his hands on his hips, just like my mother was doing. We knew that we were in big trouble for sure. so that we could scoop up the cake. After we cleaned up the cake mess, we had to mop the floor. Our mother stood close by to supervise the task.

When Grandpa came back into the house and asked about the cake, he had something to say. We knew that he would. "Who dropped the cake on the floor? Was that you boys?"
We were still cleaning up the floor when I looked up and reluctantly answered, "Yes, sir, my brother and I dropped the cake on the floor. We didn't mean to do that. It was an accident."

Grandpa said, "After all the trouble Grandma went through to bake that cake, and now look at it. What a waste." We were almost in tears when Grandpa turned to go back outside." Now we were going to get it for sure.

When we got home that afternoon from the farm, our Dad lectured us. He talked about us arguing and struggling over the cake. The cake seemed to be unimportant. It was the disagreement over who was to carry the cake to the table that was important. He mentioned the results of our dispute and the destroyed cake. Dad emphasized the effort that grandma had gone through to prepare that cake.

My brother and I received our disciplines, but it was not in the way that we thought. There was no willow switch for us. We were denied dessert for two Sundays. We could not even touch the pie or cake container at Grandma's house ever again.

My mother baked a German chocolate cake and took it on the next trip to the farm. My brother and I did not partake that Sunday in any desserts. We were still on probation at that time.

The adults had a good laugh about the cake for several years. My grandma even laughed about the cake. For years after that, every time we ate dessert at grandma's house, she would laughingly say, "Don't drop your cake." My brother and I were able to laugh about the incident years later. I think this is where my brother and I received our first family nicknames of Licky and Sticky.

Grandpa's Candy

MY GRANDFATHER LIVED AND WORKED ON A FARM JUST ABOUT all of his life. My grandmother also grew up on a farm. They were hardworking people who came from hardworking people. They were also first-generation American citizens whose parents had come to America in the eighteen hundreds. My grandparents made their living sharecropping and dryland farming, and most years, they did well. I have to give them credit. They were solely dependent on the weather to bring the rain at the right times and dry up at the right times so that they could have a successful crop.

There were times when their income wasn't very good. I remember Grandma telling me that they didn't make a dime for three consecutive years. Now those were some lean years for their family.

I can't imagine watching a crop burn up due to lack of rain and not enough moisture in the ground. That had to be stressful.

Despite the bad years, my grandparents always had their perks, as limited as they may have been. It's not that they were flowing with so many extras, but they had a couple of them. I remember that they always went to town on Saturday to pick up a few groceries from the store. They visited their farming friends, especially when they knew one of them was sick. Most of the time during that visit, they would enjoy a cup of coffee at the friend's house along with a piece of homemade pie or cake. If I went, my dessert would be served with milk instead of coffee. I can verify that the farmer's wives knew how to bake pies and cakes. They were simply delicious.

Now Grandpa had his own rules as far as when a family came to visit. We would usually visit on Sundays and have a massive meal with about five to eight people at the table. Someone was always there to visit them on the weekends. Grandpa expected those who came and stayed for a meal to bring something that they could put in the freezer or prepare for that day to eat. Sometimes it was meat, perhaps a couple of loaves of bread, some canned goods that they could serve at a later date, a gallon of milk, a can of coffee or tea, a pie, or a cake.

Bringing a contribution of food was practiced at every gathering that several people attended. An enormous quantity of food was brought for and prepared at the family reunion and on the first weekend of August to celebrate Grandma's birthday. My grandparents' twelve children and their many grandchildren came to celebrate. They barbecued brisket, chicken, pork, and anything else that others wanted to put in. There was always plenty of good food to eat and kids to play with. Their boys would bring musical instruments and play, and we would sing old ballads and songs. We always had a good time at my grandparents' house on the farm.

One of my grandpa's perks was chewing tobacco. He always had a carton of Brown's Mule plug chewing tobacco on hand most of his life. He kept a box of it in the kitchen cabinet, and after I became an adult, I always brought him a carton. I brought Grandma something that she could use. She didn't chew or dip, so it had to be something like perfume. Once I brought her a colorful apron with her name embroidered on the front of it.

Most of the farmers and ranchers that I knew back then chewed tobacco in one form or another. It was a common thing in those days to see a farmer, rancher, or one or more of their workers with a pouch of tobacco in their pockets. I remember some of the guys from high school having a can of snuff in their hip pockets while working the fields or with cattle.

My grandparents farmed about 250 acres. They grew cotton, corn, and some form of grain like maize. Some of the farm animals were given some of the corn grown on the farm. They always had a cow and a hog or two. Their work never seemed to end. I can remember riding on a tractor with my uncle while he was disking a field. Even he would chew tobacco when he was working, as did some of the others while at work. Again, it was common then.

During the summer months, Grandpa would hire some of the local kids from my school who were old enough to work to help pick his cotton crop. I was too young to do that when he was still having his crop picked, but he let me try it one time when I was about twelve years old. I don't know how those guys did that job, as it was very difficult and that sun was hot. It didn't take me long to learn to wear a hat while on the farm so that I could avoid a sunburned face. Those guys were tough in those days.

Grandma always cooked huge meals consisting of meat, potatoes, fresh garden vegetables, and desserts. After everyone finished eating and the visiting was over it was time to clean off the table and store leftover food. After cleaning up the table and kitchen, the adults would take a nap. As far back as I can remember, they always took a nap after the noon meal. After the evening meal, Grandpa had the same routine. On warm-weather days, they sat outside and caught a cool breeze. They didn't have air-conditioning in that old farmhouse. Grandpa would go out on the front porch, sit down on the steps or the porch swing, take his Brown's Mule chewing tobacco out of his shirt pocket, and take a bite of it. He would sit there and enjoy some quiet time while spitting tobacco. When I was there with them on the farm, I helped Grandma clean up the table if no one else was there.

Then I went out and sat with Grandpa. That was his routine every single time. The only exception was if it was a cold winter day. Then he would get his chew and sit in a rocker or another chair.

Every time he took that plug of tobacco out of his pocket and I was around, he would wave that plug of tobacco under my nose and ask, "You want some candy?"

Every time he did that, I would take a good whiff of that tobacco and say, "Eew, not me. That stinks." Grandpa would laugh and go outside to chew his tobacco.

One summer day, I spent some time on the farm with them, and everything was just like it had always been. Their routine started by withdrawing water from the cistern in a three-gallon milk pail. Grandma would boil it, strain it, use it to cook with, make their morning coffee, and make a pitcher of tea.

Rainwater tea tasted better than tea made from city water. I can still taste Grandma's rainwater sweet tea poured from a metal pitcher. After that, we gathered eggs from the chicken house, bring them in, and wash them off. We placed them in an empty egg carton and put them in the refrigerator. Then breakfast was cooked. It consisted of fried eggs, bacon, homemade sausage, toast, homemade jelly or jam, and coffee. When they still had a cow, we milked it every morning and put the milk in the refrigerator. The fresh cow's milk was used for cooking, baking, and sometimes drinking. I tried some of that milk once, but it didn't taste like store-bought milk. Sometimes Grandma would boil some of it, strain it, and let it cool. Then she would add a teaspoon of sugar or honey to sweeten it, and I would drink that. It was rare for me to do that, but one had to improvise when the store-bought milk carton was empty.

I can say this: Grandma and Grandpa were two of the most consistent people that you would ever want to meet. They were as predictable on most things as the sunrise or sunset. Their meals were always just as consistent. Grandma could cook, and all of their kids could too. I remember getting to their home late one Friday night. We had to wake them up to let us in the place. One of the first things Grandma would ask after the hugs and handshakes were over was, "You want something to eat. I can fix it in no time."

My reply was always the same at that time of night, "No, no, Grandma, thank you. We ate something on the way down here." Then she would go and turn down the bed.

I remember when I got married. After the honeymoon, I brought my wife to visit my grandparents. As usual, we drove a great distance and arrived at the farm at about ten o'clock at night. They were already in bed and asleep. They were retired from being farmers, but they still lived in a rented house across the highway from the farm.

They lived several miles from town. There was a tiny town about three miles away, but there was only a post office, a barbecue place, and a few houses there. The town grocery store had been closed for several years. The original county courthouse was there. The town hadn't grown very much. The fact is that people moved away—many to the new county seat.

They had an old dog that barked when we arrived and woke them up. I saw the porch light come on, and we got out of the car. I called out to Grandpa when we exited the car so that he would know who we were. We received the usual greetings: hugs from Grandma and a handshake from Grandpa. We sat in the living room. Grandma offered to cook something, but we refused and went to bed.

Although they had no air-conditioning, the nights would cool off. They lived about sixty miles from the coast, and at night, they got that coastal breeze. All you had to do was open the windows in the bedroom, and I guarantee that you would be reaching for the covers along about midnight. I slept like a baby that night.

The next morning, I could hear Grandpa walking on those old wood floors in that old farmhouse. He would walk up to the bedroom door, stand there for a minute or so, and then he would walk away. Grandpa did that two or three times before it finally got the best of him. He slowly opened the door and peeked in.

I raised my head and then said, "Yeah, Grandpa. What's up?"

He replied, "Breakfast is ready. It's six o'clock. I let you sleep in."

Grandpa closed the door and walked back into the kitchen.

My wife said, "Is he serious? Is it really six o'clock?"

Yes, he was serious, and it is six o'clock. "They have probably been up for an hour, and Grandma has already cooked breakfast. I can smell the bacon and sausage."

When we got to the kitchen, Grandma said, "I told him not to wake you up. You guys were probably traveling all day to get here.

Sleeping in until six o'clock." She chuckled. "Did he wake you up?"

"Not really, Grandma. It's nothing that a little coffee won't cure."

Grandma asked, "Are you ready to eat some breakfast?"

"Give us a few minutes to go to the bathroom and wash the sleep out of our faces, and we'll be ready." Grandma was already putting the eggs in the frying pan. That was the last thing, as everything else was ready. My wife straightened up her hair, and I washed my face and combed my hair. We ate a hardy breakfast that morning and spent the day visiting other relatives in the area.

We decided that the next time we went to visit them, we would get there just before supper and get to bed early so that we could get more sleep. We laughed about that occasion for years.

When I was about thirteen, I got brave one day and decided that if Grandpa put that chewing tobacco in my face and offered me some of that candy, I was going to take some of it. So we ate a lovely evening meal, I helped Grandma clear the table, and she ordered me outside with Grandpa. So there we were sitting on the steps of the front porch. He reached in his pocket, and with a laugh, he said,

"You want some candy?"

I said, "Yes, I believe I would, Grandpa. How does it taste?" With a surprised look on his face, he took out his pocket knife and cut me off a tiny piece of his Brown's Mule plug chewing tobacco. He said, "The first time you chew, it doesn't taste very good. You'll get used to it after a while. Grandpa handed me a small piece of tobacco. He instructed me to put it between my teeth and spit everything out. "Don't swallow any of the juice."

I did just as Grandpa said. I bit down on it with my molars and began spitting. I tried to spit like Grandpa did, but I couldn't do it. At that time, it didn't matter. I felt like I was ten feet tall. I was sitting there on that porch step and chewing tobacco with my grandpa. I felt like a grown-up who had $1 million land in my lap. The tobacco did not taste like $1 million in my mouth. After a few short minutes, I began feeling a little dizzy. The world started spinning around, and I couldn't make it stop. I looked up at Grandpa and said, "Am I supposed to be getting dizzy?"

He quickly said, "Spit it out, spit it out, and come over here." I spit the tobacco out, and Grandpa washed my face. He went into the house, got a glass of water, and told me to rinse my mouth out with it. I did. Later, he said that I turned three shades of color: first pale, then pale white, and then blue. I was one sick little boy for a little while. I set the glass down and became sick at my stomach. I gagged a couple of times and thought I would vomit, but I didn't. I was still dizzy. My head was spinning around like a merry-go-round.

Grandpa told me to keep rinsing my mouth out. He also said, "Don't tell Grandma."

"Okay, Grandpa. Am I going to be sick for very long? I feel dizzy, and everything is spinning around."

He said, "You'll be okay in a little while. Maybe you should lie down on that bench over there."

As far as Grandpa's instructions not to tell grandma, it was too late. She came to the kitchen window about the time I was getting dizzy. She came out with something for my stomach, and I took a tablespoon full of it. She then said, "Go in the house and lie down for a while until you felt better." I could hear her chewing out Grandpa for giving me the chewing tobacco. She was not happy about that.

Grandpa still thought it was funny until Grandma said again, "Don't you give him any more of that chewing tobacco. It's too strong for him. He is too young."

After about thirty minutes, I regained my composure, and I was myself again. For over thirty minutes, I had thought that I was going to die. I had been very sick and dizzy. I was still a little sick at my stomach. After I got up, I spent the next hour outside getting fresh air into my lungs. As far as I knew, they didn't tell my mom and dad about the incident. My mom would have said something to Grandpa, but my dad would have laughed at the incident. From that time until the day Grandpa died in 1986, he didn't offer me any of his candy. I didn't ask for any of his chewing tobacco either. That experience taught me a great deal. One of the lessons that I learned was to wait until you grow up before asking for an adult-sized bite of chewing tobacco.

Seriously, don't try to grow up so fast. Be a kid while you are a kid. Adulthood is complicated and difficult and full of chewing tobacco events. There's one more thing: This is not the way to learn lessons. Although my Grandpa showed poor judgment in my case, he knew I wouldn't die from it. It probably kept me away from chewing tobacco, at least for the next few years. I was too young for that experience, but I am glad that someone knew what to do to make me feel better.

As far as I know, neither of my parents knew about it until I was an older adult. My mother could not believe that I had taken that chewing tobacco. She did know Grandpa had always kidded around with his grandchildren about his chewing tobacco. I had been the only grandchild who had accepted Grandpa's invitation to take some of his candy. Why did I have to take that candy?

Roy E. Staggs

Harry's Truck

ALMOST EVERY WEEKEND, WE SPENT TIME ON WHAT WE called the farm. Now the farm was 178 acres of land in a rural area of East Texas. WR and his wife purchased the property as a getaway for their family. It eventually became a retirement property. The property sat on the banks of a creek with a hill on one end. From the top of the hill, one could see the other side of the property. It was heavily wooded. If the trees were not there, one could see the entire property from that advantage point. It was a beautiful sight, even with the trees.

WR's son-in-law Ray had a well and a septic system constructed on the property. Next, the family built a barn and purchased a tractor and other equipment. The family constructed fences around the home's site and the entire property. It would be a quiet place to live.

After WR and his wife retired, they built a house on the farm property and moved there permanently. WR thinned out the trees on the property and planted coastal Bermuda grass. Ray helped on the weekends. They cleared the underbrush, and the property began to take shape.

The following summer, the family added cattle to the farm's property. WR started small and grew the herd over time. At the peak of the operation, the family had amassed forty-eight head of cattle.

The hobby farm gave the couple something to do in their retirement years. As time went on, they added a vegetable garden and a large front porch.

The property had taken shape, and it looked like a typical small-ranch operation. WR, Ray, and sometimes RJ, spent the summers baling and storing hay for the winter feed. A typical weekend consisted of feeding cattle, repairing fences, and constructing cross fencing. Other activities included taking cows to the vet or the sale barn.

Next to the family's hobby-ranching operation, another couple who had retired to the country lifestyle lived. They built a lovely brick home. They also had cows and a hobby-ranching operation. They also grew a vegetable garden, as most rural families did.

Harry was a retired civil service employee who managed his income well. He and his wife enjoyed a comfortable lifestyle in their retirement years. Harry managed his thirty-eight-or-so-acre ranch and tended to his cows. The two neighbors helped one another when necessary and shared meals.

Now Harry liked to have a nice truck. He kept one for approximately three years and then purchase a new one. This particular year, Harry purchased one of the new diesel-engine trucks. This vehicle was new in the market for half-ton pickups. He was so proud of that new truck.

One Friday night, the phone rang at Ray's house. WR needed help loading a bull (Bullie) and taking him to the sale barn. Bullie was a registered Beef master bull. He was usually good-natured unless he was upset.

Bullie had been getting out of the fenced pasture and chasing Harry's cows. Harry called a couple of times to report that the bull was in his pastures. WR herded Bullie back to the right pasture where he belonged. WR repaired the fence, and things would start all over again. After the fourth time the bull broke the fence and chased Harry's cows, the family thought it best to sell the bull. Ray felt that Bullie would get out, walk down the road, and be struck by a passing motorist. The situation was one of liability.

Ray arrived early that morning. Upon his arrival, WR and Harry were sitting at the kitchen table enjoying coffee. After they had talked for a little while, they proceeded to connect the trailer to the truck. WR's truck was in the shop. Harry offered his new truck to pull the trailer. Ray's truck had the incorrect hitch. Ray offered to go to town and get the correct one, but Harry volunteered his vehicle again.

Harry, bragging about his new truck's abilities, said that his truck could pull that trailer without difficulty. Ray offered to get the correct hitch again, but Harry insisted. WR believed Harry wanted to see how well his new diesel truck could pull the trailer.

Harry backed his truck up to the trailer and assisted in connecting it to the trailer. Harry was particular about his truck and boasted that he knew more about ranching than anyone there. Harry backed the trailer up to the loading chute. Bullie had spent the night in the coral, and he was ready to be loaded. Bullie was not in a good mood. It appeared that he knew what was going on.

Now the trailer used in this operation had two compartments. There was a middle gate to either keep the cows forward or back from the front. The gate could remain open to allow cows to roam, but that was not the correct way to haul cattle. The son-in-law suggested that they close the middle gate until Bullie was loaded.

Harry responded, "You think that bull can jump out of the trailer?"

The son-in-law answered, "I think Bullie is upset and could probably do just that."

Harry looked at Ray and said, "Boy, I know what I am doing. Hush and go get Bullie into the loading chute."

Ray said again, "That bull is upset; just saying."

Harry turned suddenly and said, "Go get that bull in the chute." WR and Ray entered the coral and put Bullie into the loading chute. Bullie was mad at this point. WR had to put a Hot-Shot cattle prod to the bull to get him in the loading chute. Bullie was not happy about that. Bullie was in the loading chute, but he would not move an inch.

The bull didn't want to get into the trailer. As they slapped Bullie on the back and shouted at him, Bullie just stood there. So Harry, who was upset by this time, grabbed the cattle prod and gave Bullie a shot on his backside. Bullie responded quickly and furiously. Bullie shot out of that loading chute, kicking and snorting.

He went into the trailer, over the trailer's front rails, and into the bed of Harry's new truck. Then he climbed onto the cab of the new truck, onto the hood, and out of the property's front gate. It happened so fast. Bullie was out that gate before anyone could take a step. Now Bullie weighed over eleven hundred pounds. His weight alone could damage almost anything.

The top of Harry's new truck was crushed and the hood as well. Harry couldn't even get the driver's door open. He was beside himself. Harry realized the mistake that he had made by not closing the middle gate of the trailer. It was plain to see that Harry's new truck was damaged extensively.

Bullie ran down the oil-top road and then stood there as if he were admiring the damage to the truck. Ray walked through the pasture and opened a gate that faced the road. Ray called to Bullie, and as if Bullie understood, he walked slowly and gently through the gate and into the pasture. As Bullie passed through the gate, he looked at Ray, snorted a couple of times, and quietly went about his way. Bullie walked up to the fence close to the truck and stared at WR, Ray, and Harry. If bulls could talk it appeared that Bullie was saying, *Wanna try that again?* He had wanted out of that loading chute, no matter what it took. No one was going to argue with that bull. Harry drove his damaged truck the short distance home and called his insurance company. Ray purchased the correct hitch for his truck the following week.

The next weekend, they connected the trailer and took Bullie to the sale barn. WR and Ray had no trouble loading Bullie into that trailer. Of course, the middle gate was closed. Bullie brought a good price at the sale barn. WR no longer had to worry about the bull getting out. Ray and WR built a pipe fence along Harry's property line. As for Harry's truck, the insurance company took care of that situation. In a show of good faith, the family paid Harry's insurance deductible. The sale of the bull made it easy to pay that deductible.

For a long time, Harry was not happy about the incident, but eventually, he made amends with his neighbors. Harry never offered his truck to move cattle again. He ultimately apologized to Ray for his temper. Ray gracefully accepted, and they remained good neighbors for years. Harry wasn't satisfied with the repairs to his truck. He traded it in for a new one. It was a Chevrolet, and it had a diesel engine.
WR and Ray bought a new bull a few weeks later. It was another registered Beefmaster. He was gentle most of the time. The bull

eventually grew to be about a thousand pounds. The bull was stubborn, and it could be a little cantankerous. They named the bull Harry.

Jake the Accountant

JAKE WAS ONE OF THE BEST ACCOUNTANTS IN THE COUNTRY. All the people in the town of Anywhere, USA, wanted Jake to do their taxes. He was so well versed in the tax laws that his friend at the IRS called him on occasion for advice. In all the years that Jake did taxes, none of his clients were summoned for an audit by the IRS. Now there are people like Jake in every country in the world. Jake may or may not be a Christian, but he is well-liked by all his friends and family members. He is especially liked by his clients.

Jake was also an avid reader and a good speller. When he was a child, his parents had to frisk him to find hidden books in his jacket or pockets when he left for school. The teachers always liked him because Jake did well in school, paid attention, and made excellent grades. He could look at a page, and the misspelled words seemed to jump off the page. All his teachers commented on what a good student he was. Teachers and his parents commented on how well-behaved Jake was. Jake could sit in a classroom, read a book, and listen to the teacher at the same time. One would say that he was a multitasker.

One time, his teacher saw him reading at the back of the room. She called on him to answer a question that she proposed to him. In an instant, Jake told her the correct answer. From that point on, she didn't have to call on Jake, unless no one knew the answer.

Jake's parents were so proud of him. He spent the first semester of school reading and studying all his books. By the time the second semester of school came around, he was familiar with the entire school year's lessons. I do believe that the boy had a photographic memory. His brother and sister questioned how he could make straight As in school without bringing a book home to study. Some people thought it was because he could remember the entire book.

His parents often questioned Jake on his schoolwork. Jake was always on top of his homework. Some thought he was a genius. Jake's specialty was numbers. Mathematics came so easy to him. A college professor once remarked that math was a language. If a student spoke the language, they were good in math; if not, they did poorly in math. Jake didn't know about the college professor's comment. He only knew that he could add, subtract, multiply, and divide three-digit numbers in his head by the time he was in third or fourth grade.

Jake had another talent after he became an adult. He could figure out the logarithm of the lottery numbers. When he was twenty-one, he won two lotteries consisting of $25 million. Jake didn't want to take advantage, so he put the money in a trust. Jake wanted to earn his way through life.

As a high school student, he dreamed of having his own accounting business that catered to the wealthy. His dream also included doing taxes for the less fortunate for a highly discounted fee —sometimes for nothing.

Jake won a full-ride scholarship to the University of Texas to study mathematics and accounting. When he took the entrance exams, they could offer him nothing in mathematics that he could not do. So Jake entered the first semester with twenty-one credits. During the summer between the first and second semesters, he purchased five accounting books from two graduating students. That summer, Jake read through all five of them. When school began, he knew the contents of all five books.

When the second semester came, he challenged every accounting class that the university offered. Jake added fifteen additional credits to his collection, beginning the second semester. The following summer, he purchased every English and science book that he could find. Jake studied them all summer. In the third semester, he challenged every science and English course that he needed to graduate. His studies proved successful. Jake graduated with honors after only three years of college. Jake took the CPA exam that summer and passed it on the first attempt. One could say that he was a genius, and one would be correct.

When he had been fifteen years old, he had gotten an unprecedented 169 on his IQ test. Things only got better over time. He was such a gifted child and adult also. His test scores in mathematics and accounting were among the highest any Texas university had seen. After Jake graduated and became a CPA, Jake's dream of having his own business came true one year out of college. Jake spent many hours doing taxes for some of the wealthiest people around.

Multimillionaires from every walk of life called on him to do their taxes, advise them on taxable donations, and help them avoid paying so many taxes.

He further specialized in tax-sheltering money, especially in foreign bank accounts, which were untouchable by the US government. His genius in income taxes was unsurpassed. Even the IRS was impressed. He was even offered a field-office director's position with the IRS, but he refused. Jake believed that he could make more money on his own.

Now Jake never forgot the less fortunate. When his dream came true, he fulfilled his promise to help the less fortunate and hired two accountants to do taxes for them for free. They were always swamped at tax time. Many of the less fortunate would return and pay the highly discounted fee after receiving their refunds. Jake became popular with all walks of life in his town. I know that they appreciated his business sense and efforts.

Jake would go on for over twenty years preparing tax returns and handling investments. Jake also taught math to help math-poor students where he lived. He felt so disheartened when a student didn't speak the language. But Jake had a solution for that. He pioneered the development of teaching methods for students who didn't speak the language. He taught the language so that they could understand most of it. Even those who didn't speak the language could speak enough to pass a basic college course. His students loved his teaching methods.

Throughout the years, Jake made a holy fortune in his occupations. By this time, Jake expanded his business to handle other assets for the wealthy. He made even more money for himself and his staff. He did pay his staff well. Some of the wealthy people that he worked with paid him a handsome tax-deductible retainer for monitoring their incomes and expenses. The wealthy granted Jake unprecedented access to their financial affairs so that he could help store away their money and invest it in areas that would prove to be very profitable. Of course, Jake made an additional bonus each time he made more than the estimated earnings and tax-sheltering funds.

The tax firms that initially did tax returns for those wealthy people were jealous of Jake. But he soon was in their good graces. Jake didn't mind sharing his tax knowledge with others. His thought was that there was enough business to go around, so why not help them make money. Of course, he charged a fee for those services. Jake made money when they made money. He was correct. There were enough money-rich people to go around. Jake's business enterprises developed a vast clientele, and his staff of thirty accountants followed Jake's learned skills in accounting and mathematics. Everyone in the business made tons of money, but Jake made the most.

Every time Jake made any investment or tax-preparation money, everyone made money. Jake's clients were impressed with his extensive knowledge of tax laws, asset management, sheltering funds, and so on.

One of Jake's friends once asked him if he thought that he could run for Congress. The Federal Bureau of Investigation wanted him to help track down criminals using his knowledge of world banking and finance. Being the accountant that he was, Jake refused the offer.

He declined every position that the government offered him, saying that he was not a politician. He knew that he could make it on his own.

He did need wealthy clients to make the business work, but he had a database full of them. No wealthy person went uncontacted. Jake also contacted current tax firms. Some refused, but eventually, they came around to Jake's way of doing business. Sometimes he hired a tax accountant who worked for the wealthy person or firm just to get the business. That strategy paid off in a big way on several accounts. Wealthy people could see the results of his investing and sheltering after the first tax year.

Jake did make millions, but he was smart about his money. He didn't splurge too much. Jake lived in a typical neighborhood, drove a midsize SUV, and wore suits from the Men's Wearhouse. Jake always said, "No high-priced suits for me." Everything he bought was on sale or discounted. He never paid full price for anything, as far as anyone knew. He searched the papers and online stores every day for deals, discounts, and free stuff.

He was seen at Dillard's buying clothes for their 65 percent off sale. One of his friends saw him there and asked what he was doing.

Jake replied, "Buying some new clothes. I'm not paying full price for anything. Who would pay sixty-dollars for a shirt I can buy for thirty? Certainly not me. You should follow my advice, buy at the sale, and save your money for retirement." Jake was right on that point. These actions were what impressed most people about Jake, especially his clients' wives. He was just an average guy who didn't waste his money or his talents.

Now Jake did have a wife. She was just as frugal as he was. She shopped just like Jake did. Please don't misunderstand me. They had nice things. They just didn't pay a lot of money for those nice things. They did have nice clothes—tuxedos, gowns, and so on.

Jake's wife drove a nice car, but he had bought it used. It was a Mercedes, but he purchased it from a client who was trading it in after fourteen months. Jake's wife loved the car.

There was one thing that Jake and his wife didn't buy discounted: going out to eat at a nice restaurant. They enjoyed nice restaurants with good food. Many times, they would meet clients at those fancy restaurants so that Jake could write that expense off for his business. Many times, the clients did the same thing. It was a given that someone would benefit from the evening out besides enjoying the food. Jake put a considerable amount of the money that he earned into foreign banks, mainly in Switzerland. He also kept money in banks in the United States, but only for business purposes. After all, the IRS could monitor his business enterprises anytime that it wanted to. On occasion, it looked at his financial situation but found nothing out of the ordinary.

After about twenty-five years of operating his businesses, Jake was worth a whopping $900 million in US dollars. He was one of the wealthiest accountants in his circle of friends or the United States.

Even his business staffers made hundreds of thousands of dollars a year doing their best to ensure that those wealthy people got theirs. As far as anyone knew, they did get their share.

Jake decided to retire from his business enterprises after twenty-five years of actively making money. His business staff bought his business along with his business model for $10 million. The company was worth much more, but Jake didn't want to take advantage of the people who had helped him make hundreds of millions of dollars over the years. He wanted them to be rich just like he was. They went on to make more and more money. About four years later, his staff sold the business. Their pockets were lined with more money than they could spend in two lifetimes. Everyone that Jake was associated in business with made vast amounts of money.

Now Jake moved to Switzerland for about a year, and then he and his wife just disappeared. It was like he had dropped off the face of the earth. He had always wanted to live incognito. Jake was no longer concerned about making money. There was plenty to live on comfortably for the rest of his life. He was now living the life of Riley and enjoying every moment of his newfound life. No longer would anyone call him in the middle of dinner and bug him about tax concerns or while on vacation.

Jake had sacrificed much of his former life catering to others and making money. Now Jake was well paid, but he was getting a little tired of everyone always wanting a piece of him, especially those wealthy people whom he filtered funds from. Yes, Jake took a little more than his fees from those wealthy people, and they didn't even realize it until it was too late. Jake figured that they could spare the money because they had so much of it. In all his taking and giving, he never filtered money from someone who couldn't afford it.

The people that he grew up with and his close friends in his hometown, he did their taxes for free. This included his parents and siblings. Jake had a standard. He never took anything from anyone who wasn't worth over $100 million. Jake took his fees and extra money from the profits made through investments. The wealthy investors using Jake's company did not lose their principal investments. As far as the IRS was concerned, it was happy to take money from the wealthy, even though it didn't receive a dime.

As far as Jake was concerned, he was living abroad somewhere and even going to church to give thanks for all that he had received. Perhaps he was even sipping a margarita or maybe a glass of vintage wine and enjoying fine foods at a nice restaurant. When Jake was asked for his name to make reservations, he used his new identity. The doctors did a fantastic job of his and his wife's reconstructive surgery. Even the FBI was unable to find or identify him and his wife. Maybe it was because FBI agents made millions too, along with some members of

Congress. They were all on his staff. It does pay to know the right people in the right places and plan well for the future. By the way, the FBI said that Jake hadn't violated any laws by taking the money. Well, there is one federal law that he violated. A spokesperson said the company might be cited for overcharging for professional services. A conviction is not likely. It appears that all financial records on those matters have disappeared. The FBI said that it had them but that they were now lost. An agent must have misfiled them in a paper shredder in the back room. Three years later, Jake repented and returned every dime to its rightful owners. He returned to the United States under his and his wife's assumed names. He went back to teaching students the language of mathematics. They were a captive audience, and they clung to every word that he said. They love the stories of how he made his millions. He has a comfortable place to live, three meals a day, and a nice library to read in.

Because the records of his events could not be located, Jake was not prosecuted and neither was anyone else. Jake now works as a financial consultant for the FBI. His wife still shops at Dillard's when it has its 65 percent-off sales' event. She no longer has the Mercedes. Instead, she drives a BMW. They live comfortably on Jake's lottery winnings. He still has it.

Lessons Learned

I DON'T KNOW WHY, BUT I ALWAYS WANTED TO BE A SHERIFF'S deputy. Even as a child when I watched cops and robbers' shows, I wanted to be the cop instead of the robber. All the kids in the neighborhood knew my side of the fence early on. Sometimes I played the robber to see what it was like to be one. I did not become a full-time cop or robber.

After I became an adult, I went to work at a local municipal governmental job. It was a promising career for me, and it gave me a chance to be a public servant in my own way. I did, however, have an opportunity to become a reserve officer. Our small town didn't have much crime going on, so I rode with the sheriff's department on the weekends. I put my name on the list for a rider, and it was always accepted. Some possible reasons were that they were always shorthanded or someone was always sick or on vacation.

My name was on the list for the following Saturday night. It was summertime and hot, so I wanted the nights because they would be a little cooler. Summer days could get up to a hundred degrees quickly, and standing there directing traffic in the hot sun was nothing to brag about. That pavement could be about 130 degrees on the surface. The idea was to have a comfortable pair of shoes on.

Leather shoes looked good when they were all polished and shiny, but they made a person's feet extremely hot when standing on the pavement. Also, chasing a suspect on an asphalt pavement with leather soles on was the pits. They were slippery as well as hot.

The phone rang at my house at about eight o'clock on Friday night. The sergeant of the sheriff department's patrol asked me if I would work the day shift that Saturday. I would be riding with a seasoned deputy, and he could teach me a great deal. I agreed to work with this officer. I knew him from high school. We used to hang out at the sheriff's sub-station and talk with the deputies. He was a good guy and taught many of the deputies their trade. Besides, he wasn't quick to blame others. He was also well-liked in our community.

I showed up at six o'clock the next morning, and I was ready for work. The seasoned officer drove into the parking lot at about the same time that I did. We walked to the door together, giving each other the customary handshake and good morning. The patrol sergeant told us about a rash of burglaries that had occurred in some of the warehouses. These warehouses were in our district. We were told to be on the lookout for any suspicious activity.

Both of us enjoyed our traditional donut and coffee in the squad room before our shift's briefing. This was where you found out what made an officer tick. Some interesting conversation took place at the break-room table. I couldn't believe some of the stories that I heard. Some told of close encounters of the wrong kind while others talked about their weekend family adventures. During these conversations, I first heard the saying, "Bringing a knife to a gunfight." Some of their stories were hilarious.

After the briefing, we hit the streets. The first item on the agenda was to fuel the vehicle. We needed a full tank of gas to start the shift. There was no way to determine when we would get back if it turned out to be a busy day. This full tank would last the entire shift. One had to be careful when fueling the vehicle. Sometimes, a deputy who was playing a joke would lock the gas pump's handle in the on position and place it back in the holder. If one was not careful when the pump was started, it would automatically begin dispensing fuel before one was ready. Many deputies spent the entire shift smelling like gasoline because it had splashed on their pants.

We started our patrol in the warehouse district immediately after fueling the vehicle without incident. We were in the warehouse district about fifteen minutes before we received a disturbance call. We responded to the call, and a second unit was sent as our backup. After arriving, we went to the door, knocked, and went inside. Our backup arrived about a minute after we went inside.

When our backup came, he excitedly jerked the door open and rushed inside. It kind of startled me when he came bursting in without saying anything. One moment he wasn't there and the next he was. It was a wonder that one of us didn't draw our weapons as his sudden entrance. We settled the complaint without an arrest or citation and promptly exited the house.

When we went to the car, we talked to the other officer about his sudden entry into the residence. His answer was, "I just never know what I'm getting into, so I'm prepared for anything." Donna, my riding partner, explained that a move like that could have provoked the resident. The officer was quick to act, but he did not look before he leaped. One never wants to provoke a incident, especially a domestic one.

Two months before this incident, the deputy and his reserve had worked a possible silent-alarm call at the data-processing facility.

They entered the business through a broken glass door. After walking around for a few minutes, they entered the computer room. This room housed the company's mainframe of computers. As the deputies moved around, one of the computers started up.

Reels were spinning, and lights were flashing. The deputy and his reserve were both startled, to say the least. Here they were all alone in a quiet, dark, and large room. Then, all of a sudden, the computer started up with a sound that they had never heard before. The deputy drew his weapon and fired before he could think. That bank of computers never knew what hit them, but it did know what to do. It made another weird sound and then fell silent. The sound was quite loud, and the backup officers heard and saw the whole thing. The county still has not settled that claim.

Donna explained these things to me. She said that when the thought process is skipped, actions come first. That was when the training took over. It only happened when an officer was fired at or in an event that required a quick response. That was the time to be fast and sudden. She pointed out that we always needed to watch, look, and be prepared for anything. She also said that being prepared did not mean that we acted out before we assessed the situation. She pointed out that we should respect others and that they would show us respect in return. The day turned out to be a hot one. The sky was clear, and the sun was intensely bright. A good pair of shades was necessary for that day. The ole eyes could not stand that sun for very long. Both of us had our shades on as we began driving back to the warehouse district. We had gone about a mile when another radio call came in.

This time, it was a possible burglary at one of the warehouses that we were supposed to be watching. We turned on our warning lights and sped to the area. Our backup was the same unit that had backed us up at the disturbance call.

Three blocks before arriving at the warehouse, we turned off our warning lights. As we entered the alley's parking lot, we noticed a small pickup parked about a hundred feet down the alley. I copied down the license plate's number and auto's description and called dispatch to run the license plate. Donna took her shotgun with her as we exited the car. I was armed with only my service weapon and a five-cell flashlight. Before we entered through back door, which was unlocked, we turned our handheld radios' volumes off so that the burglars couldn't hear any radio traffic. This would alert the burglars of or presence.

The door being unlocked was suspicious as it was supposed to be locked with a deadbolt. I looked up at the door before entering and noticed that it had an alarm on it. Both of us surmised that it must be a silent alarm because no warnings had gone off when we had arrived. We entered slowly and cautiously because we couldn't see a thing for a few minutes. We inched our way in with our backs up against a cinder-block wall. The warehouse was huge. We could hear noises as if someone was moving around near us. We continued to move silently, so as not to warn the burglars of our presence.

We didn't know if the suspects were armed. Most of the time, burglars didn't carry firearms, but one never knew. I pulled out my weapon and inched myself behind Donna and along the wall. We knew that we were close to finding the suspects. We didn't use our flashlights. We didn't want to give the burglars any sign that we were there. The building was so dark.

At about the time our eyes began to adjust to the darkness, a loud sound came from behind us. This sound could be recognized by any police officer, seasoned or not. The loud sound was the slide action of a pump shotgun going off behind us. I knew that the suspect had heard us, made his way behind us, and was going to shoot us. My heart was pounding, and my stomach felt like it was in my throat.

As soon as we heard that sound, we quickly turned around. I pointed my weapon, and Donna aimed her shotgun right at the person behind us. As we prepared to fire, we recognized the person behind us. The person was our backup. He had bolted in through the door, racked a shell into the chamber, and proceeded down the hall without knowing where the burglars or we were. The backup deputy saw that Donna had an angry look on her face.

Donna turned around and loudly said, "Police officers, come out with your hands up *now*." Two men came into the light of my flashlight with their hands up. Donna and I escorted them to our squad car. These two were suspects. When we had cuffed and searched them, I asked them, "Is anyone else in the warehouse?"

They said there was no one else, but a detailed search had to be performed anyway. People are not always truthful, especially when dealing with police officers.

When the backup deputy came outside, he was pale. I thought he was ready to faint. I placed the two prisoners in the car and called in the signal to dispatch. "Two suspects in custody."

Donna grabbed the other deputy by the arm and escorted him to his patrol car. She began chewing that young deputy up one side and down the other. She completely lost it for a few minutes. I stood there watching it as a learning event. The patrol sergeant arrived at about the time Donna had finished chewing out the other deputy.

Although Donna was upset, she calmed down quickly. After Donna calmed down, the patrol sergeant was brought up to date on our situation. She also informed him of what the other deputy had done on his arrival. All three of us were so glad that we recognized the deputy in time to avoid firing our weapons. That could have been a terrible event. In an attempt to hurriedly leave the scene and go home, the backup deputy backed his patrol car into a guard post, doing severe damage to his unit. He spent an additional hour at that scene while another officer was called in to investigate that accident. It took the other officer only fifteen minutes to investigate it while social distancing from the other deputy. Donna and I promptly left the scene of the accident in the patrol sergeant's hands so that we could take our prisoner to the jail for processing.

I learned a few things from that event; in fact, all three of us did. First, backup should always notify the first officers to respond when backup arrives on the scene. Second, you should wait until the backup arrives *before* entering the building after a burglar. This way, everyone knows the situation. The most important lesson that I learned was to always take the necessary restroom breaks while on duty. Our backup deputy learned that one at this event. The last lesson learned was always taking the appropriate steps to avoid an accident, especially when you need to go home.

Donna was promoted to detective in the Criminal Investigation Division. She is now the captain over that division. As for me, I teach at the police academy. The first lesson that I teach is the importance of taking appropriate restroom breaks. I also teach gung-ho rookies how to enter a warehouse correctly when looking for a burglar. My job was made easier when I invited Donna to relate the warehouse burglary incident. My rookie officers have no problem understanding these lessons.

The gung-ho deputy quit the sheriff's department two years later and after a brief encounter with a German shepherd in a private residence. The report stated that the deputy had rushed into a residence to assist a city officer with a burglar call. The police officer and the owner had the dog calmed down and secured by the time the deputy arrived. When the deputy rushed into the residence, the dog thought he was the burglar and attacked. The deputy was not seriously injured.

The gung-ho deputy moved to California, where he began working in motion pictures. He earned a modest living portraying burglars and gung-ho police officers on made-for-television movies. After a year of acting, the former deputy was given a pet as a studio gift. He now owned a schnauzer named Max. Max is nonviolent.

A year later, Max became an actor in his own right with his own television series. The former deputy/actor was now Max's sidekick and always got into trouble. Max had to rescue him time and time again. Max had a second sidekick. Her name was Maxine. She was a lovely schnauzer, but she couldn't stand to be around the former gung-ho deputy.

The former deputy didn't play a role in the television series. He is now the caretaker and housekeeper of Max, Maxine, and their pups. All of them live in the deputy's house. Isn't it odd how things turn out in life? The sheriff is looking for a replacement for the gung-ho deputy. Anyone want to be a deputy?

Living the Moments

IT WAS A CALM AND OVERCAST NIGHT ON THATTUESDAY WHEN I arrived home to relax after a long day at work. After my dinner of leftovers, I sat down to unwind from the day. I was watching reruns on the television while enjoying a glass of iced tea and a small snack. I had watched about three shows when I became sleepy.

I had already taken my bath and changed into my gym shorts, T-shirt, and socks. You may think that is an odd way to dress when going to bed. There is a simple explanation for that. I was a member of the volunteer fire department for my fair city, and when I had to wake up in the middle of the night to go on a call, there was little time to put on my pants, shirt, socks, and shoes and head out the door.

Instead, I had bunker pants and boots already positioned so that all I had to do was step into the shoes and pull up the straps on the bunker pants. Then I was ready to head out the door.

I had attached a spare door and car key to my bunker pants. My coat was in the truck. A flashlight and a small fireman's bar wrench were in my coat pocket, along with my gloves. My helmet was in the seat beside my coat. If awakened in the middle of the night, I could be out the door in two minutes. Preparedness was the key.

I was in bed when it began to rain, which made me even more comfortable and sleepy. I'll bet it only took five minutes for me to fall asleep and drift off to my dream worlds. To hear the gentle rain falling on the roof was so soothing. I didn't remember hearing about rain in the forecast. Who cared if I knew it or not; it was raining. We needed the moisture, and it helped me sleep.

The sound of thunder and lightning woke me up. I tried to go back to sleep, but I was awakened again to the sounds of sirens in the distance. The wind was picking up speed, and it began to blow furiously. I could hear the rain and roar of the wind in the trees around my house. The sirens sounded for about a minute, stopped, and then sounded again. Three times those sirens went off. It meant that we had some kind of civil defense warning in place. That was the signal at the time: three consecutive siren blasts. Hopefully, that would wake up most people in the city and give them fair warning of some impending danger.

About that time, I heard a limb from one of my trees crack and fall in the side yard. I jumped up, ran to the window, and looked outside. The tree limb had missed my house by about five feet. I couldn't see much because it was very dark, but I could see the large limb lying beside the house when the lightning flashed. The wind was furious and gaining speed with every second.

I heard hail hitting the roof and bouncing off my city pickup and the sidewalk in front of the house. My personal car was inside the garage, my city truck was in the driveway, and my pickup vehicle was under the attached carport. I wondered for just a second how the city pickup would stand up to the hail. I knew it would take a beating. It would be okay as long as the hail didn't break any windows. The clouds looked dark with a green tint to them. I could hear the wind blowing fiercely and I could see the tree limbs bending under the stain of the wind.

I picked up the phone and called dispatch to see what was going on. I could tell that the dispatcher was in panic mode already. She screamed in my ear, "Take cover, take cover, tornado on the ground, tornado on the ground." Then the phone went dead. I assumed a tree limb had broken off and took down the phone line to my house.

But I hadn't heard another limb fall. I then thought the wind had blown the lines down somewhere else and that the phones were dead in the whole neighborhood. The storm had caused the telephone and power service to be disconnected.

I quickly put on my fire-department bunker pants, fished my wallet and keys out of them, and then took my flashlight from my nightstand. I headed for the nearest closet in the center of my house. At about that time, the lightning cracked and hit the transformer near my house. The power went off. When I glanced outside one more time, I could tell that the entire neighborhood was dark. People who lived in the tornado belt of Texas knew that they had have a secure place to go during these emergencies and needed an extra flashlight and bottled water there as well. I also had a crowbar in my closet in case I had to pry a board off to get out.

I could hear a roar that sounded like a freight train outside. It became louder and louder. I knew a tornado was getting closer and closer. It was in my neighborhood. There was no telling how much damage it would do. I could hear things hitting my house and my city truck.

As I sat there in my closet, I hoped that the tornado would pull back up into the clouds before it reached our street. More things were hitting my house. Another limb broke off one of my trees. It had sounded like it hit the home near the carport. My city truck was undoubtedly taking a beating from the hail and flying debris. There was no telling what they would look like when this was over. I just hoped the houses in my neighborhood would stay in one piece. The homes in this neighborhood had been built some thirty years ago. Although they were well-built, no wood structure could withstand a tornado—at least not one that I had ever seen.

I sat there for several minutes listening to the violent wind and weather. I opened my heart and offered a prayer to God for those who must have caught out in the terrible weather. I asked God for his protection for everyone in our fair city. I kept praying as I wondered if my house was going to explode into a thousand pieces. Two windows blew out in the living room, and I could hear the loud sound of things flying around in my living room. I heard my pictures and other things hitting the walls. The wind was so loud that I literally could not hear myself think. I bowed my head once again because my neighbors were in imminent danger from this storm. One was elderly, but she had been through it before. I was certain that she knew what to do. There were two young couples with children and others that I didn't know in my neighborhood also. Surely they had heard the sirens and taken cover. This was my prayer for them.

After what seemed like forever, the wind died down, and quietness fell around me. Just like that, it was all over. The tornado had passed, and now it was time to emerge and survey the damage. I stumbled out of my closet and went down the hallway to my living room. I thanked the Lord that my house had survived the storm. I flipped the light switch on, but nothing happened. I couldn't imagine that the power had come back on that quick, but I had to know for sure. I shone my flashlight around and looked in the other rooms of the house. The tree limb I heard hitting my house had fallen through my living room window. The wind had scattered most of the things off my shelves, but my house overall was okay. There were things scattered around my living room. The damage didn't bother me that much. I could replace material things. Everything in a bookcase was gone except a picture of my mother. It was still there, unharmed. How could everything be off the walls and that picture still be standing in the bookcase? I couldn't figure that one out.

I opened the front door and looked around for a few seconds before going outside. I didn't know if there was a live power line on the ground or not. I wanted to be sure before I stepped outside on the porch. I went around the house and checked the electrical and phone lines that went to the house. They were still attached. I shone the light toward the street, and those electric lines were still in place.

I shone the light toward the transformer one house down from mine, and it was gone. The lightning had destroyed it. There were no live power lines on the ground that I could see. I checked out the damage to the roof and the outside of the house. Two windows had blown out in my living room. A tree limb now stuck through the open windows. My carport was damaged.

I opened my garage door and retrieved my chain saw. I cut the tree limb that was protruding into my house off. I pulled the limb out of my window and off my carport. My city and personal trucks were unharmed. A few dents were on the hood and roof of the city truck, but both vehicles were in running condition. It was pleasing to learn that the windows in the vehicles were unbroken.

I looked across the street as my elderly neighbor was emerging from her hiding place. She had heard the tornado and taken cover. I went over and asked her if she was OK, and she nervously replied, "I'm

OK. How about you?" I was in good shape. There was no visible damage to her house, and her car was in the garage. I checked the houses on both sides of my house, and I could see slight damage to the roofs, but I couldn't see any structural damage. I called out to each neighbor and asked if that person was all right. Each one responded with the thumbs-up sign. I went back to my house. All was well, so I began dragging limbs out of the street so that emergency vehicles could pass. I cut and pulled the limbs away so that I could move my vehicles when it was time to leave for work.

When I got back inside, I heard my fire-alarm box sounding off. I listened for the location and type of call. I drove off into the night, dodging tree limbs on my way. The call was to help place a plastic covering on a nursing home's roof. We would also assist the nursing staff in moving patients to other rooms if necessary. Fortunately, none of the residents or staff was injured.

While in route to the nursing home, the fire chief called on the two-way radio. The chief asked me to stop and remain at the fire station in case another call came in. The two paid firemen had left the station and gone to the nursing home with a fire truck and an ambulance. I would have to pass the fire station on my way to the scene, so I was the logical choice.

When I arrived at the fire station, the power was still on, even though my neighborhood had no electricity. I closed the bay doors and went inside to the dispatch room where the phones and radios were. At about the time I entered that room, the fire phone rang. The police dispatcher answered the phone, and I listened to the caller report power lines down in another part of the city. I informed the dispatcher that my neighborhood was also out of power. The police patrol officers and other volunteers were dispatched to block off streets until the electric company could respond and secure the area.

Another volunteer arrived at the station, and it was just in time too. The fire phone rang again. As I listened to the caller, I could tell he was terrified. The dispatcher and I tried to calm the man down. We needed to understand the nature of the call. We were able to obtain the address, and the other volunteers and I responded in the backup ambulance. When we checked in on the radio, we advised the chief of the station's vacancy.

The call concerned a pregnant woman who was having her baby. Ordinarily, this would not be such an emergency, but the couple had a problem. They were trapped inside their home, and they couldn't open the front door. When we arrived, I could see that tree limbs had hit the house and jammed the front door. I grabbed the fire tool from my jacket pocket and broke the window's glass in the living room. I crawled inside while my partner pulled some of the tree limbs from the door. With the assistance of the patient's husband, we cleared a path through the limbs. We were unable to get the stretcher through, so we walked the patient to the ambulance. We were able to get her to the hospital before her baby was born. That was a good thing.
Although we knew what to do and how to do it, we liked it better when the doctor was doing the delivery.

We arrived back at the fire station just in time to roll on a home accident. Apparently, a man was cutting away limbs from the driveway and cut his leg with the chain saw. His wife called. She was frantic to get help to stop the bleeding. We responded with three people in the ambulance. The paid fireman and I attended the patient in the box while a volunteer drove to the hospital. We were able to stop the bleeding, and doctors were able to save his leg.

The night ended for me at 6:05 a.m., just in time to take a shower and report to my city job. I was tired but ready to do my duty again. I called my insurance company and asked them to handle my home. I went home for a couple of hours to secure my house against would-be vandals. It had been a long night, but this was where it counted. It was about people coming together to help one another in their hour of need. We had done this many times in the past, and we would do it many more times in the future. Whether it was a vehicle accident, a health-related situation, a fire, a tornado, a flood, or other calls for help, we were there. In the many years that I had worked with the volunteer fire department, I had responded to many calls. I responded to 327 calls in all. I helped deliver two babies, worked thirty-two major accidents with injuries and seven major accidents with deaths, rescued two girls from a burning automobile, and fought countless fires of all kinds. We even worked a train derailment that had polyvinyl chloride on board. At one house fire, I fell through the roof of the burning house and landed on the coffee table in the living room. I would have burned to death if it were not for the gallant rescue efforts of my fellow volunteer fireman. They went into that burning house and rescued me quickly. It was a good thing that I was wearing a self-contained breathing apparatus.

I worked a call one day when only three of us there were there. A house on the edge of town had smoke flowing from a window. I was the first one on the scene. The fire truck arrived about thirty seconds later. I grabbed the red line from the side of the truck and proceeded through the back door. I was on my hands and knees attempting to locate the source of the fire. I was in that house about ten feet. I thought my backup was right behind me, but he wasn't. Before he could enter, the fire took oxygen and created a back draft. The door slammed behind me, crimping the hose and shutting off my water supply.

Firefighters are trained to be conscious of their surroundings at all times when entering a burning structure. The rule is to never go into a building alone. There should always be someone there for support and assistance. I had noticed a window on the left side of the door as I had entered the house. There was a small table there, so I quickly dragged it aside. I took three steps back and then plowed through the window with my self-contained breathing apparatus on and in full firefighter's attire. I landed on top of the fire chief. One could say that he broke my fall. No one was injured in the ordeal. I had been burning up in that house because the temperature was about 130 degrees. I was in full gear too, and I got very hot very quickly.

When a firefighter is driving a fire truck, he must always bear in mind that water is onboard—sometimes as much as fifteen hundred gallons. Now water weighs about 8.34 pounds per gallon. The water adds significant weight to the apparatus. Also, the water cannot be tied down or secured; therefore, it will move and surge while driving. As the truck slows, speeds up, or turns, the water moves adversely. Baffles are installed in the water tank to reduce surge. These baffles do not eliminate surge, but they do help.

We were taught the use of the lights and siren and when to deploy them. When an emergency vehicle responds to a call, the lights and sirens are in place to warn other motorists that an emergency vehicle is approaching. Texas laws say that a driver must yield the right-of-way to those emergency vehicles. However, when approaching an intersection, one must approach with caution. Although the other vehicles are supposed to yield the right-of-way, the emergency vehicle does not automatically have the right-of-way. When the emergency vehicle has a stop sign or red light, it must yield to other approaching vehicles until they yield the right-of-way to the emergency vehicle. Then it may proceed through the intersection.

One day, paid firefighters were responding to an ambulance call. When a second call was received (a car fire), the dispatcher sounded the alarm and summoned a volunteer force to respond.

One volunteer did just that. The man exited the fire station and proceeded toward the call with sirens blaring and lights. As the truck approached a red light, it slowed while scanning for traffic. A driver, who thought he could beat the fire truck through the intersection, proceeded without yielding.

The fire-truck driver saw the vehicle, slammed on the brakes, and turned sharply to avoid hitting the automobile. This maneuver caused the water in the tank to surge, thus causing the fire truck to overturn in the intersection. The volunteer notified the dispatcher that he had been in an accident so that police could respond to his location. The volunteer was not injured, but the car that was on fire burned to the ground without a firefighter present.

Firefighters are involved in some challenging conditions. After fighting a structure fire, their boots are dirty and many times muddy, their coats are dirty and smoky, and their equipment is also in the same condition. After each call, the units, hoses, and equipment must be cleaned up and made ready for the next call.

One day, they had worked a structure fire. It hadn't been a total loss, but there would be a substantial insurance claim in the structure.

All the firefighters returned to the station to clean up everything. One of the firefighters backed the unit up to the doors, stopped, got out, and then went inside. At about that time, it began to rain. When a break in the weather came, he went outside to park the unit inside. When he cranked the engine, he didn't push the clutch pedal completely down. The truck began to move backward. Paying no attention, the firefighter changed gears and pulled forward as another firefighter opened the appropriate bay door.

The firefighter backed the truck into the correct place. When he got out of the vehicle, he slipped on the sideboard. His boots were wet and still had mud on them; therefore, this made them slippery. As the other firefighter assisted him, he asked, "What are you going to do about the door?"

He responded in a quick temper. "I am going to close it before the rain starts again." The other firefighter asked him about the other door. "What other door?" the one replied.

"The one you just backed the fire truck through." With a puzzled look on his face, he walked to the other side of the station and saw the damaged door. He then went to the fire truck and saw the glass all over the tailboard of it.

The firefighter who had seen the accident was a volunteer. The firefighter who had backed into the door was a paid firefighter. The volunteer left and went home. A month later, the volunteer was at city hall when the city manager approached him about the door. The volunteer replied, "The incident was explained in the report." The city manager responded by saying, "How do explain backing through a door in broad daylight?"

"What are you talking about, sir? I didn't back into a door. Your paid firefighter did." The city manager motioned him to follow him to his office. He showed the volunteer the accident report stating that the paid firefighter and the volunteer had backed through the door.

It had been raining. The firefighter's boots were wet. His foot could have easily slipped off the pedal, and before he regained control, the truck damaged the door. Why had he blamed the volunteer? There was no explanation for that lie.

Two days later, the volunteer confronted the firefighter. After a heated discussion, the paid firefighter said, "You signed the report. Prove it."

The volunteer said, "Did you know that Bobby was standing right beside me when you backed through that door? If I need to, I will call him to testify. Now what do you have to say?" The case was closed and filed away.

Through all the calls that I made, I never wrecked a fire truck or an ambulance. I was only seriously injured one time when a fire hose blew off the truck and struck me. I had no broken bones, but it cost me thirty-five stitches and four days off work. Other paid and volunteer firefighters were injured while performing their duties, but none were life-threatening.

I am so glad to have been of service to others in my community. It is service to others that brings people together in a community. Everyone is watching out for each other and lending a helping hand. You see that this is one of the things Christ talked about when he said to love your neighbor as yourself. Many others did the same thing in our community and so much more. All of us were so glad to put our needs aside to help others. To be able to do these things is undoubtedly a gift from God. All the inconvenience, danger, discomfort, loss of sleep, and pain were worth every minute of it. If I had nine lives to live, I would spend them all just like this—helping others in their hour of need. God bless those who love their neighbors.

Texas Barbecue and Fugitives

NOW TEXAS BARBECUE IS SOMETHING MOST PEOPLE LOVE, even if you are not from Texas. There are many different recipes and flavors, and people prepare it in different ways. Other states do a good job of preparing barbecue, and it tastes good also. They have their pride just like Texas does. Texas seems to have a lot of those places scattered around. At the moment, I cannot think of a county in Texas that doesn't cook and serve barbecue, in one way or another.

If you want to find a cop in the city, go to a donut shop, especially when the early morning shift change comes around. In the county's rural areas, cops can be found at any barbecue place, especially at lunchtime. Many of them wait until they are off duty because barbecue can be messy to eat, especially the ribs. They are, as we say in Texas, finger-licking good.

Other states also serve excellent barbecue. Believe me; we have tried them all. It's good food, especially with two sides, a glass of iced tea, and dessert. Trust me on this one, it is tasty. You may want to consider going on a short diet before indulging in barbecue meal, especially the desert. That cobbler is also finger-licking good.

One hot summer day, a car pulled into the parking lot of a rural Texas county sheriff's department. A middle-aged man exited his rented vehicle and went inside. He identified himself as Brian, a police officer from a city in the northeast. His accent gave him away.

They knew immediately that he wasn't from Texas, not that it is a bad thing. The people in the north can recognize a man from Texas in the same manner.

Brian was carrying a briefcase with wanted posters regarding a jail escapee from his jurisdiction. The sheriff's deputy sent the officer to a detective who was familiar with Brian's bulletins and case. Brian was looking for a fugitive who had escaped from custody a couple of weeks earlier. He was a convicted felon and believed to be armed and dangerous. The fugitive was also believed to be in the area, or perhaps he had passed through the area on his way to Mexico or Central America. Brian and the detectives discussed the issue at hand for a few minutes. Deputy Joe called Deputy Sam on the phone and asked him to join the meeting. They concluded at the end of the meeting that the fugitive had relatives in the area and possibly in that county.

He was most likely hiding in one of his relative's homes. The three lawmen proceeded to interview people in the area who might have come in contact with the fugitive. He was most likely holed up and waiting for the right opportunity to leave. He could still be living with one of his cousins. Evidence found the next day confirmed this theory. They also determined that the fugitive could make a run for the Mexican border at any time. As close as they were, the escapee could cross the border that day, if he hadn't already done so. They had to decide quickly how they would catch the fugitive.

As the three discussed the case extensively, they came up with a strategy to capture the escapee. Brian knew for sure that the escapee had relatives in that county. According to witnesses in other states, his trail had led them to South Texas. Deputy Sam saw the bulletins on the escapee and called Officer Brian when deputies found an out-of-state, stolen car matching the one in Brian's jurisdiction. Brian determined that the escapee stole the car in an adjacent city after escaping. The case was beginning to heat up, and they needed to move on it before they lost the trail. According to authorities, the escapee would have no problem committing other serious crimes if he was not captured soon. Anyone who stood in this man's way could be seriously injured or worse. They needed to find this man and take him into custody before he hurt another person. At least, that was their plan.

After a week of exhausting searches and inquiries, all three officers believed that the escapee had found his way to Mexico. They needed proof of this. His relatives informed the officers that he had been there but had left. The relatives said that they had no idea he had committed horrible crimes and was an escapee. The escapee's family did not know where he was. They believed he was going to Mexico to live with other relatives.

The three officers made the trip to the border, checked the videos, and thought they saw him in some of the footage. This was disappointing, to say the least. If they had missed him and allowed him to escape, he could come back anytime, commit other crimes, or perhaps commit crimes in Mexico. No one knew what the outcome would be.

It was noon when the three started back to the county. Deputy Sam offered to stop on the way back. Officer Brian wanted to eat lunch. He wanted to try some of the Texas barbecue that he had heard about. People had told Brian that if he came to Texas, he had to try some of the delicious barbecue. They agreed to go back to their home county to eat lunch. It was about one o'clock when they
arrived in the county. Officer Brian asked if they could eat at the place they had passed on the way out of town that morning. Brian went on to again explain that he had always heard of Texas barbecue but never tasted it. Officer Brian wanted to treat himself before he left to go back

home. The local deputies knew precisely where to get such a meal and decided to grant Officer Brian his request. It would turn out to be a real treat and ordeal—well kind of.

This barbecue restaurant was well-known and ordinarily crowded during lunchtime. It was a hometown favorite, especially for the oil field employees and local business people. The building was rustic and located on the edge of the city. Because it was one o'clock, they hoped that most of the customers were back at their workplaces. When there were too many people in the building, it was noisy and difficult to talk about the case. The building looked like an old barn on the inside because the wooden rafters were exposed. The outside was no different. The roof was made of tin, and the porch was made from planks. It was indeed a rustic-looking building.

The older man who owned the business had bought an old feed store and turned it into a restaurant. The benches and tables were all made of wood and stained to perfection. Western art was hanging on the walls, and a bar counter was at the back of the building. It was a traditional Texas barbecue establishment. Customers were served at the table most of the time. On special occasions, they also had a cafeteria-style counter.

The three officers arrived at 1:15 p.m. They exited the sheriff's vehicle and walked across the gravel parking lot. Brian commented that he knew of no business that looked like it in his county. Officer Brian commented on how rustic the place looked as they stepped up on the porch. The two deputies assured Brian that looks only indicated the restaurant was frequented by many, which made the restaurant well-known. They assured Brian that the food would be delicious and plentiful.

Deputy Sam said, "Brian, you will have no regrets about eating this fine barbecue. Only one piece of advice, get plenty of napkins. You will need them." Officer Brian asked, "Is the food greasy? Is that why we need more napkins?"

"No," Deputy Sam replied, "it's not good if you don't get some on your shirt or pants. That's the reason for the extra napkins." Officer Brian chuckled and said, "Not many people here today. Must be late for lunch. I feel like I am starving."

The restaurant had about ten people seated at various places. Heavy wooden tables made of oak with captain's chairs were located in the center of the large open space. The outer walls had booths for customers. The floors were also made from oak planks, which were stained and varnished to perfection. The tables were made the same way. Someone had put a lot of work into the place, even though the building had been an old feed store about forty years earlier.

The building was quiet enough for the officers to talk. They found a table where at least two of the officers could see both doors. This positioning was normal for police officers. The server came to the table before anyone sat down and asked what they wanted to drink.

All three ordered iced tea. All three officers went to the bathroom to wash their hands. When they returned to the table, their glasses of iced tea were already there. The server was at another table talking to a customer.

Deputies Sam and Joe sat down. When Officer Brian sat down, his jacket became entangled with his weapon. Officer Brian tugged on his jacket to no avail. Officer Brian grabbed his gun to release it from his sports jacket. As he tugged on the jacket to free it because he thought he was sitting on it, they heard, "Bang!" His .38 special revolver had fired. It was a deafening sound.

None of the officers made a move or a sound. As they looked around the room, they could see that some of the customers had ducked under their tables. The officers could see others looking around to find out who had fired a gun in the restaurant. Immediately, everything had become quiet. You could have heard a pin drop in that place. The three experienced law-enforcement officers looked astonished. They said and did nothing.

One of the deputies said, "Must have been a car backfiring." The other officers nodded their heads as if to agree. The other customers regained their composure and finished their meals. Five minutes later, the only people left in the building were the three officers, the server, and the chef. They thought that the other customers had needed to get back to work immediately.

The server returned to the table and said, "Those jets make a loud boom when they break the sound barrier, don't they."
One officer said, "Yeah, I guess they do."

After the server left their table, Officer Brian looked down at his chair and the floor. There was a hole in the chair the size of a dime and another one in the floor. It was a good thing that there were no pipes under that part of the floor. It would have been a shock to see water spraying up through the floor at their table.

After consuming delicious barbecue and a glass of tea, they ordered a piece of peach cobbler with ice cream for dessert. As the server brought the check, she asked Officer Brian, "Do people from the North leave good tips."

Officer Brian answered, "Why yes, we sure do." Deputies Sam and Joe forked over money for their share of the meal. The server took the money for the meal and also a large tip from Officer Brian. The server leaned over close to Brian's ear and said, "Congratulations, Barney, you shot a hole in my floor. But that's all right. You should have seen the look on that guy's face when a cop shot the commode out from under a guest last year." The server was laughing as she left the table. Officer Brian walked up to the server and gave her ten additional dollars as a tip. The cost of tip was now more than the meal was. Officer Brian thought it was worth the money, especially now that he didn't have to write a report of the incident. The deputies didn't say a word. They quickly exited the restaurant.

When the officers returned to the car, Officer Brian asked, "Did an officer really shoot the commode out from under a guest?"

Deputy Sam answered, "I sure did. With a .357 Magnum. I couldn't hear a thing for two days."

Officer Brian looked at his suit and said, "I have ruined a good pair of slacks and a sports jacket. I smell like gunpowder. I need to go to my hotel, take a shower, and change clothes. Is there a place to buy a new sports jacket and slacks?"

They took Brian to a local establishment, and he bought new clothes—a complete set. Brian commented as he returned to the car, "What a way to end a trip to Texas. We didn't capture the escapee, I shot a hole through a chair and the floor, and I ruined a sports jacket and a pair of slacks. Could this get any worse? I didn't know Texas barbecue would be that expensive."

Deputy Joe said, "Hope you left her a good tip?"

Officer Brian said, "More than you know."

Officer Brian left that afternoon to catch a plane back to his home county. He was wearing his new clothes. As he boarded the plane, he felt like he had lost his best friend. He was going home without the fugitive, and his boss would not be happy about that. In fact, the sheriff had already called Brian's boss and told him about the lost escapee.

The day after Officer Brian left, the escapee was captured. Deputies Sam and Joe made the arrest without incident. According to the report, the escapee had left his cousin's house, was walking down the street, and was trying to catch a ride south. When Deputies Sam and Joe saw the escapee, they immediately stopped the vehicle, got out, and approached him with guns drawn. The escapee was happy to surrender to the deputies of his own free will. He had no gun, but he was well fed. The fugitive was worried that someone would shoot him. He told the deputies that someone had shot through the floor at him where he had been hiding. The escapee ran and hid, fearing that law enforcement had a shoot-on-site order out on him.

Deputy Sam told the fugitive that the shot had come from a trigger-happy officer from up north where he had escaped from. The fugitive commented that he knew he was wanted for escaping from custody but that he didn't know he was wanted dead or alive. The fugitive was told that the trigger-happy officer had already gone back to his home county. The escapee was relieved to know that no one had been trying to shoot him on site, especially when he had been trying to eat Texas barbecue under the restaurant. The escapee also commented that perhaps he should have eaten lunch inside the restaurant instead of under it. That may have been safer than almost taking a bullet through the floor.

The server that waited on the officers was the escapee's cousin. She had brought him food, and at night, the escapee had stayed in the server's garage. To keep the authorities from capturing him, he hid under the restaurant and only came out when it was dark. The restaurant sat about four feet off the ground on one end, and it could be easily entered and exited. The escapee's cousin had slipped out the back door and handed him food. Then he had sat under the building and eaten.

When the gun had accidently discharged, it had missed the escapee by only six inches. In fact, the bullet shot a hole in the glass of iced tea, which was sitting on his right side next to his leg. He quickly exited the area without his lunch, went to his cousin's house, and waited for her to get home from work. When she got home, he informed her about the bullet narrowly missing him. She called one of the deputies the next morning to come get her cousin. She felt that her cousin would be safer in jail, especially if Officer Brian was going to extradite him. The escapee feared Officer Brian was still there, so he took off walking. That was when Deputies Sam and Joe spotted him.

The two Texas deputies were later awarded medals of valor for capturing the escapee without incident by the department where Officer Brian worked. They were also written about in the sheriff's association's monthly magazine. Deputies Sam and Joe had taken part in the extradition of the escapee and received their medals.

Brian was not happy with this situation because he thought that he should have been awarded a medal also. His sheriff disagreed with Brian's opinion. Brian was later demoted and placed at a desk, where he filed reports and answered the phone. The sheriff later fired Brian for discharging his weapon into his chair at work. The bullet had ricocheted off the concrete floor and struck a picture of the sheriff as it had exited through the wall. The bullet then broke the light fixture in the sheriff's office, which was adjacent to Brian's office.

The sheriff was seated at his desk at the time of the incident. No one was injured. The chair, picture, and light fixture were a total loss to the department.

Officer Brian now works as a security guard at a nuclear power plant at an undisclosed location. He is armed and carries an additional thirty-four rounds of ammunition. As for the Texas deputies, they are still employed by the sheriff's department. Deputy Joe was promoted to captain and works with the major crimes and fugitive division. He also assists outside agencies with extraditions.

Deputy Sam was promoted to chief deputy. His predecessor was fired for allowing a prisoner to escape while eating lunch at the local barbecue establishment. Deputy Sam found the escapee hiding under the barbecue establishment when the server brought him something to eat. She was also arrested for harboring a fugitive. The charges were dropped, and she was released from custody. Chief Deputy Sam interviewed her before she was released. Chief Deputy Sam decided that she was not a contributing factor in the prisoner's escape and that she didn't know the man was an escapee. They have a mutual understanding about guns, fugitives, and Texas barbecue. She also reminded the chief deputy of the cost of replacing the toilets that had broken when they had been shot with a .357 Magnum, which a certain deputy (now a chief deputy) had carried. Thank goodness no one was injured in either incident. One never knows about guns, fugitives, and Texas barbecue.

The Man Next Door

WE WERE LIVING IN THE SUBURBS OF A LARGE METROPOLITAN city at the time. It was a hustle-and-bustle city with large subdivisions of track and cookie-cutter houses. Our subdivision was home to middle-class working people with diverse backgrounds. There were retired people, those who had small businesses, and others who worked for government agencies like social security, law enforcement, etc.

My parents were no different from the rest of our neighborhood. Dad worked on the management team of a car dealership and put in long hours at his job. My mother worked part-time until I was thirteen and my sister was fifteen. She went to work at a full-time job the summer that I turned thirteen. My sister and I were on our own at home. My sister was the nerdy type who read books and viewed social media. I was the rowdy type, so I spent a lot of time outdoors.

My best friend was Alex. His real name was Alexander, but it was shortened by his school friends early on. Alex and I spent the summers running and playing. We spent many hours all around the neighborhood with other school friends and played games. We built things in our backyards and developed games so that we could use the things that we built. Alex's dad built a tree house in their backyard for us to play in. Both of us had binoculars and spent a lot of time playing spy games.

The man who lived next door seemed strange. He had moved in right after the school teacher who lived there took a job in another school district. She put her house on the market in May and sold it two weeks later. Our new neighbor didn't have a wife or children that we could see. He didn't have a dog or cat that we could see either—no family, no pets, or anything. On occasion, he had a visitor or two, but that was all. He didn't socialize with the neighbors, but he was friendly enough. He would speak when spoken to, but he didn't engage in conversations with his neighbors. Once, our basketball went over the fence, and he was kind enough to return it after we knocked on his door. One could say that our new neighbor was a quiet man who didn't want to be bothered or bother any of his neighbors.

He was a well-dressed man. His shoes shone like they were new. I asked my dad about the man's shoes one time, and he said the man had probably been in the military at some point in his life. The man wore a suit with a tie when he left his house. Anytime Alex and I saw him, he was always wearing nice clothes. He also drove a new Chevrolet Suburban with dark-tinted windows. It looked like one of the vehicles that you see politicians or famous people using when traveling to keep anyone from knowing who they are.

Now Alex lived across the alley from our house. We would talk on the phone, but we also had walkie-talkies that worked well from house to house. One afternoon, we were in the tree house looking through our binoculars at the neighborhood. We noticed that the man who lived next door had his shades pulled up in one of the rooms at the back of the house. We focused on him for a few minutes. He had what appeared to be a microphone like the cops use in his hand. He was talking into it just like they do on television. We thought that was strange. Why would he have a two-way radio in his house? At this point, we were confident that he was a spy of some kind. We watched him for a few minutes talking into the microphone.

After about three or four minutes, he closed the blinds. Many afternoons, we watched to see if his blinds were open. The majority of the time when we peered at his window using our binoculars, the blinds were closed. But on occasion, the blinds were open. Then we watched as he communicated using his two-way radio.

Alex, Freddie, and I began a spy operation that summer by watching the man next door. We documented the man's activities.

We noted when he left the house and when he came home. We also noted when he used this two-way radio. Since Freddie lived next to Alex, he could easily watch from his upstairs bedroom window. I did the same from my bedroom, but Alex lived in a single-story house, so he had to get in the tree house to spy. All of us had strategic locations to watch the man next door.

We did notice something about his activities. He would sometimes leave and be gone for several days at a time. Then he would be home for two or three days. We thought that he was going on vacation, but this happened about every two or three weeks. We thought that was strange. I thought he was a government agent working for the FBI, the Secret Service, or perhaps the CIA. That made sense to us. He didn't have a job like our parents did. They left early in the morning and came home that evening. The man next door did not have that routine.

We didn't tell our parents about our spy operations. We thought they would stop us from watching the man next door, so we kept quiet. We must have used thirty or more pages of notes from our spy booklet that summer. We spent a great deal of time watching our neighbor to no avail. We didn't have any more information at the end of the summer than we had had at the beginning. Some spies we were. All we knew about the man next door was that he left and came home. He also spent several days away from home and then stayed home for two or three days. What could he possibly be doing there? One thing was for sure was that we were lousy spies and detectives. We proved that by reviewing our notes at the end of the summer.

We had a good time that summer spying on our neighbor and playing detective. Alex, Freddie, and I decided that we would treat ourselves to chocolate shakes. We rode our bikes to Baskin-Robbins and ordered a large shake for each of us. We sat down at the half-moon shaped booth in the corner so that we could see who came into the store. Alex was in the middle of a big gulp of chocolate shake when he suddenly stopped. He turned white as a sheet, and he couldn't talk because his mouth was full of ice cream. Alex nodded his head to tell us to look at who was coming into the store. We quickly looked up, and there was the man next door. The man was in his usual suit, shined shoes, and colorful tie. We almost fainted. We couldn't believe it. There he was in full public view. We hadn't seen him in public before. We were stunned.

The man ordered, came over to our table, sat down, and asked,

"How are my neighborhood spies doing today?"

We looked at him, and all three of us said simultaneously, "Huh?" I thought we were in serious trouble. How did he know? What gave us away? Who was this man who saw us spying on him? How did he pull that one off?

He asked, "Find out anything, boys? Let's talk while we enjoy our shakes. You are not in trouble, boys."

We chatted for thirty minutes about how delicious the shakes were and made other small talk. The man did most of the talking while we listened. Before he left the booth, he invited us over to his house to see his radio set. We were unsure of this guy's intentions. Was he inviting us to his house to silence us? What did he have on his mind?

We rode our bikes back to my house. My mother was home, so we let her know that the man who lived next door had invited us to see his radio set. She was surprised that we wanted to see it, but she approved our trip into the unknown. We wanted my mom to know where we were just in case we didn't come back.

We were terrified to knock on the man's door. The man answered the door and invited us in. He offered us cold drinks. We were thirsty after devouring our large chocolate shakes. We went to the backroom, which had been a bedroom at one time. There he showed us his radio set. He was an FCC licensed ham-radio operator. He said that he had always been fascinated with radios. Radio were his hobby. He had friends all over the city and state whom he talked to just about every evening.

He opened his closet door and pulled down a photograph album. He explained that he was a retired special agent for the United States Secret Service as he opened it. He showed us a picture of his wife and two children, who had been in Maryland getting things together so that they could sell their house. The house had just sold on the previous day. He said that his wife would be there in two weeks. His children were grown. They had come by a couple of times to check on him. "You guys saw the two people that came to visit two or three times over the summer, right? They are our grown children.

He went on to explain that after retiring, he started his own business. He protected important clients on various business trips all over the country. "I guess you boys noticed I was gone for several days at a time?" he asked. We nodded. "Do you guys have any questions for me? Something you always wanted to know but were afraid to ask?"

I spoke up, apologized for spying on him, and said that my parents would be happy to meet him and his wife. I went on to say that I was sure he would like our parents. The other guys agreed. I had one further comment before we departed. "You must have some neat stories to tell. Could you tell us some of them sometime?"

He said, "I would be glad to do that, boys.

We left that afternoon with a new outlook on our neighborhood and our newly found friend. We would spend the next ten years visiting with the man who lived next door. Alex and Freddie moved away during my junior year of high school. When I graduated from high school, the man who lived next door gave me a gift I will never forget. He invited me to go with him and tour the White House, along with three of his former agents. We had a blast.

I do have one piece of advice to offer. If you don't know your neighbor, knock on the door and introduce yourself. You will be surprised to know who they are.

The Photograph

(Based on a True Story)

I HAD BEEN RETIRED A COUPLE OF YEARS WHEN I BEGAN reviving a book that I had started several years earlier. My job had gotten in the way of me finishing it, so I thought that I would start working on it. I was impatient and wanted to get it going again. The real reason was that I needed a purpose again in my life. Before my career ended, I had been going about ninety miles an hour. Then the next day, there was nothing. Everything came to an abrupt halt. I needed something to do, so I opened up my computer, found the book, and started working on it again.

My younger brother called me one night, and we began talking about our dad. He had found his name on a World War II website. It gave some information on the crew that he served with and the usual things like rank and position. The next day, I began looking through our dad's pictures and war information. I had had these pictures for many years. Dad had collected these pictures over a lifetime of experiences.

We knew that Dad had served in World War II and been on a crew that flew missions on B-24 Liberators. We saw pictures that his brothers and sisters had collected through the years also. We heard stories that some of his brothers and sisters told about him. Some of them were about his time in the military. We didn't know much about his war years because Dad didn't talk about it. Most veterans of that war didn't speak much about their experiences. We did know that Dad was credited with fifty-one combat missions and was awarded several medals during his wartime service. There were even a couple of news articles about him coming back home after serving in Italy.

I looked through his pictures, as I remembered seeing some soldiers in uniform sitting on camels. Those seated were all officers. In the background was one of the pyramids and the Great Sphinx.

There were other people in the picture from North Africa, who had rifles slung over their shoulders. Those men were almost as tall as the camels, and the rifles looked like a child's toy rifle in comparison to their height. My dad had kept that picture from the war and talked about it for years. Dad said that the tall people guarded their planes and called every American soldier Joe. They also said not to come back to the plane early, as they would shoot first and ask questions later.

When Dad looked at these pictures, he identified and called someone George. I knew the name from that picture only. Dad must have thought a great deal of this man, although he was about four years younger than he was. George was an officer, and Dad was an enlisted man, so they did not socialize. Officers and enlisted men were prohibited from associating by military policy.

This World War II photograph was of an aircrew during their break. The B-24 aircrews would get a week off from their combat duties to rest and relax. They would fly to a friendly occupied location outside of the combat zone. The men in the picture were part of a bomber crew that was flying missions over Europe in 1944 from Italy's bases.

It was impressive to look at those old photographs and have Dad identify the people in them. Another picture was of Dad standing in front of an airplane. He had the biggest smile that I had ever seen. I had never seen my dad smile like that.

After another long conversation with my brother, I decided to take a closer look at Dad's war information and pictures. There was something there, but I didn't know it at the time. I knew that I should take a little time from my current book project and see if I could uncover some additional information. My brother had questions, but I didn't have answers. Even our older cousins who were alive during the war didn't know the answers to my questions. At this point, Dad had passed away a few years earlier. Dad's brothers and sisters were not alive to ask. There was no one to ask and no one who had the answers that we needed. I even tried to access Dad's military records to no avail. I was in a pickle.

I resorted to the last thing that I could think of but probably should have done first. I googled my dad's name, and a website popped up advertising a book. I wondered why Dad's name would be associated with this book. As far as I knew, Dad never wrote or cowrote a book, especially about the war. That piqued my curiosity, so I clicked on the website.

A book popped up on the screen, and the pages had Dad's name on them. The pages told of a bomber crew and listed the names of all the members of the crew and the positions that they were assigned. There was Dad's name. He was listed as a staff sergeant.

He was assigned to the tail gunner's position on the plane. The book went on to describe their training and so on. I read further into the book and found that it told of a mission where my dad had shot down an enemy plane. I looked at all the pages that listed my dad's name.

I researched the author's name: George Crawford. On another website, it listed his phone number. I thought that surely this man couldn't still be alive. My dad had died at the age of eighty-six in 2004, so this man had to be at least ninety years old. He couldn't possibly be alive. With curiosity still in my brain, I called the number, and a woman answered. A brief conversation took place, and then she asked, "Would you like to talk to George?" I almost fell out of my chair. The man was still alive.

George came on the line, and I was almost speechless. I told him who I was and my dad's name. George recognized the name and asked if he was still alive. I informed him that dad had passed away in 2004. I began asking about his book and lots of other things that he answered. Then it was time to ask the most crucial question. "Sir, would it be possible to meet with you and interview you? I have so many unanswered questions about my dad during that time, and perhaps you could fill in some information." He agreed to meet, and I thanked him for his time and ended the phone call.

A few minutes after hanging up, I went back to the website and ordered two copies of his book—one for my younger brother and one for me. I knew the books would not come for a few days, but I wasn't interested in asking George about his book as much as I was interested in finding out more details of Dad's missing life during the war.

The last two years that he had been in a health-care facility, Dad had filled me in on most of the missions that he could remember and other things. I wrote down as much as I could. I wished that I had recorded those conversations so that I could replay them. I only had my notes. I even had a difficult time reading my handwriting, but I managed to rewrite them.

I booked a flight to Dallas for the following Tuesday and left to meet George and his wife at their residence. I was never so nervous in all my life to finally meet the man in the photograph. They had invited me to lunch that day, so I caught an early flight and took a taxi to their residence. When I knocked on the door, this man, who was about five feet, five inches, opened the door to the apartment.

When I looked at him, I just stood there for a minute or two. He must have thought I was some kind of idiot because I didn't say a word for at least a minute. I introduced myself, and we shook hands. He asked me if I saw his wife at the door to the building, and I said that I hadn't. The taxi had let me off at the wrong building in the complex, so I had walked up the hill to the correct one. As I hurriedly walked up the sidewalk, I inadvertently walked behind the bench where she was seated. The bench was close to the driveway, and the sidewalk was about ten feet behind the bench. I wasn't looking for anyone, and I didn't know that I should look.

George and I went downstairs, found Jeannette, and went to the dining room for lunch. We had a great visit. I enjoyed our visit immensely, but I forgot to bring the photographs that my dad had left me because of my haste. To help me remember everything that George said, I had brought along a digital recorder that could record several hours of conversations without my having to recharge the battery. That was the best thing that I did throughout the trip. We visited for about three hours before I needed to get back to the airport to catch my flight home.

I scheduled another visit with George before I left. I listened to the recordings on the flight home. Silly me—it sounded like I did most of the talking on those recordings, so I had to change my way of interviewing to get more information.

The next time that I interviewed George, I remembered the photographs. As we sat down at their table, I began pulling out the old photographs. He also produced a few of his own. I was so impressed that he had kept all of that stuff from the war. He was a multitude of information. Toward the end of this interview, I asked my lifelong question about a particular photograph—actually two of them. First, I pulled out the photograph of the soldiers sitting on camels. He explained who the people were in the picture, where they were, and what they were doing there. I didn't know any of this information. Finally, I pulled out another photograph my Dad had in his collection. I asked George about it. He didn't remember the specific date. George did identify the plane in the photograph. The plane was named *No No Cleo*.

Dad was standing there with his sleeves rolled up and a smile like he had just won the lottery. I asked George to take a look at it and explain something. Why would a soldier be that happy, as indicated in the photograph? He was in the combat zone, on foreign soil, and in the middle of a war. Why was he happy about being there? I couldn't understand why he would be smiling like that. George looked at the photograph for a few seconds and then put it down. We talked for a few minutes while he explained some things about being on their flying missions. George was a copilot on the same crew as Dad was. He moved on to become a first-rate pilot in his own right.

He had attended two years of college before the war and completed
flight school just in time to join the same crew as dad had and also in time to be shipped overseas to combat.

A few minutes went by, and George picked up the photograph. He looked at the photograph and then looked at me. A smile came over his face. I looked at him and said, "What is it?"

He was still smiling when he answered my question. "You want to know why he is smiling in this photograph? In Italy, the crews were required to fly fifty combat missions. A gunner could fly with other crews if they wanted to speed up the process, providing that they lived through those missions. Most of them didn't finish their fifty missions because they were lost on missions over enemy territory when they parachuted out of the plane. If they lived, they were captured by the enemy, and they became prisoners of war. In this photograph, your dad had finished his fifty missions, and he was going home. That was why he was smiling. He didn't have to go on another mission. He had met his combat requirements.

George answered the questions that I had had in my mind, and now I could understand all too well how they felt after completing their requirements and being ready to go home. My friends told me that I should write a book about my dad and tell of his wartime experiences to explain what it was like living with a combat veteran who suffered from PTSD. I told George about this, and he had this advice for me: "Don't think about it, just do it." So I did. It took me three years to do it, but I finally got it done.

George didn't live long enough to see the book published, but I gave his wife, Jeannette, an autographed copy in thanks for their help with the information about my dad and his wartime experiences.

I am so grateful for the information, but more importantly, for meeting a person who loved life and the Lord and had such a successful life and marriage to Jeannette, whose friendship I treasure. God bless you.

The Race

SHE WAS UNDOUBTEDLY THE MOST BEAUTIFUL GIRL IN THE entire eleventh grade. Every junior and senior wanted to take her on a date. Her parents would not allow her to date until she was a junior in high school. Her girlfriends thought she was square because she had never been out on a date with a boy. She did have classmates that came to her birthday parties and outings, some of which were at the country club where her parents were prominent members.

She had a strict upbringing. She avoided R-rated movies and television shows, which had inappropriate language or sex scenes. Her girlfriends thought that was odd and that her parents were too strict. Her friends in school knew she was on the A honor roll every semester. She always dressed appropriately and never used vulgar language. Besides all of this, she was drop-dead gorgeous. All of the boys in the school would turn, look, and take a deep breath when she walked into a room. They also knew she was now eligible to go out on a date. Every boy in the eleventh and twelfth grade was on edge. Most thought that she was way out of their leagues.

Karl and I thought the same thing, but we were going to try anyway. The worst she could say was, "No." In reality, she could say one of three things: "Yes," "No," or "Maybe." We didn't tell any of our other friends about our thoughts on the matter.

Some children mature early in life and learn respect, honor, politeness, and manners at a young age. Other children move into adulthood and seem to never learn these disciplines. My friend Karl and

I were some of the early learners. We had all these traits. The girls seemed to notice it more than the boys did. The guys that we went to school with didn't care about respect, honor, politeness, and manners. Those guys only wanted to get out of high school and into the workforce. As for Karl and myself, we had been best friends since first grade. We wanted to go to college and have good jobs.

Many of our classmates wanted to go to college too. Most couldn't afford college. Her name was Barbara. She had long blond hair, the bluest eyes anyone would want to look at, and a somewhat slender build. She could have entered the Miss Teenage America Pageant and won, if you ask me. What else could a guy ask for in life? She was smart, well mannered, and disciplined. She had a sense of humor, and she was beautiful to boot. We didn't know a great deal about her parents, other than that they were financially successful, high society, and charitable. We even saw their picture in the paper one time. It had been taken at some charity event at the country club, where they were also members. Barbara was part of that scene. Karl and I thought it might be fruitless to try, but we had to know the answer.

We were just plain, ordinary guys with good parents who loved us and cared about our futures. All in all, Barbara's parents seemed to be decent parents who were strict with their children. Barbara had a sister whose name was Kate. She was like Barbara in many ways. She had the same academic achievements, but she was different in her physical appearance. Kate was also slender, but she had light brown hair and the prettiest green eyes. She was a very attractive girl and well mannered.

We didn't think that Barbara and Kate were the only two attractive girls in the school. There were several others, but Karl and I were just attracted to Barbara. Kate was not allowed to date yet. She had to wait until the following year. Karl and I had gone out with other girls on our many double and single dates. We enjoyed the usual dinner and movie dates and Saturday lunches at the local teenage hangouts.

Both Karl and I seemed to always ask our dates about Barbara. That conversation would be short, and the answer was usually, "She's OK. We get along well, and she is good at school. Why do you ask?"

Our answers were usually, "Oh, no reason. I was just curious."

There was one occasion that Karl asked his date about Barbara and got a different answer. His date said, "Who are you out with, Barbara or me? Stick to one date at a time if you want to go out with me again." Karl and I agreed that it had been a mistake to ask, so we dropped that strategy. We didn't want the girls to think that we were only going out with them to find out more about Barbara.

One could say that Karl and I were in a competitive race to see who got the first date with Barbara. We were not the kind of guys to hold a grudge, and it wasn't about a bet or anything like that. We wanted a date with Barbara and thought, *Let the better man win*. We would let Barbara decide who she wanted to go with on a date.

Now keep in mind that it wasn't anything vulgar either. We had great respect for Barbara, and we also knew that her father would go off the deep end if anyone made any kind of gesture or language like that to his daughters. He made that clear at Barbara's birthday parties the previous summer when another student made a rude remark about Barbara in her bathing suit. He was not allowed to attend Barbara's or Kate's parties at their house or at the country club. Karl and I didn't want to be expelled from getting a date with Barbara. We knew that all the guys in our school would be jealous of us when we got the date with Barbara.

Karl made the first attempt to ask Barbara out. After school, he saw her in the hallway. He made the bold move to introduce himself and ask for her phone number. She politely denied him the number. Then he asked if she wanted to go out on a date. She looked at him for a minute and politely said, "Let me think about that, and I will let you know. I can't give you the number as it is unlisted." We knew she wanted to ask some of her friends about him before deciding. When Karl spoke to her about two days later, her answer was sure and swift. "No." We couldn't figure out why she had said no. Karl was a good guy, and he hadn't been in any trouble at school or anywhere else for that matter. I was in the same boat as Karl was. I hadn't been in any of these situations either. I was now in panic mode. If she turned Karl down, she would most assuredly turn me down also. I needed a plan.

I thought about this dilemma the entire weekend. Karl and I talked three or four times over the weekend. Karl even asked his mother about the situation, but she gave no definite answers. His mother had just smiled and said, "That's just a girl's decision to make, and you shouldn't push the issue. That will only offend her." That Monday, it would be my turn to ask, and I was so afraid that she would say no. At least Karl and I would be on equal ground. We would have to just move on and know that we were not in the same class as Barbara was. We would have to admire her at a distance. It looked like the only way we were getting a date with Barbara was in our dreams.

Monday morning came around much too soon, but there it was. The morning crawled by. It was lunchtime by the time I got a chance to see Barbara face-to-face. She was walking to the cafeteria when a guy bumped into her and made her drop her purse. I stopped and picked up the purse and asked if she was okay. She smiled and thanked me for picking up her purse. We began to walk to the cafeteria together. I spoke up and told her my name. She looked at me, smiled, and said, "Yeah, I know. You are Karl's friend."

Karl? I thought. *I am doomed for sure now.* She just turned down Karl, and now she was going to turn me down. We did the small-talk thing as we walked to the cafeteria.

I had to make one last-ditch effort to get a date, so I offered to buy her lunch and asked if she wanted to sit with me. After we stopped in the lunch line, she turned and said, "Let's get our food then see about sitting down." I took that as a brush-off or a stall tactic to let me down politely. We got our food, and I made good on my offer to pay.

When she walked to a table, she asked, "Is this table OK?"

I quickly responded with, "Yes. This will be fine." She sat down.

I walked as if to sit on the other side. She quickly said, "No, please sit here." I sat next to her. I was so nervous that I could barely hold my fork. She sensed that I was nervous and said, "Are you OK? You look a little nervous."

I said, "Yes, I'm fine. I just never sat next to anyone like you." She smiled and said, "I'm a student just like you. Relax and tell me about yourself."

I never saw Barbara sit next to anyone other than one of her girlfriends. As we began to eat and talk, I realized that she was comfortable to be around. I asked her if she had seen the new movie that had come out on the previous week. She didn't answer right away. Then

I decided to come out and say the words that I have wanted to say forever.

Before I could say a word, she turned and said, "When did you want to take me to that movie? I would like to see it. Would that be OK?" I was stunned. I almost fell out of my chair. I turned, tried to look like I wasn't about to burst, and said, "That's a great idea. I would love to see that one too. How about Saturday evening? Or Friday works too."

Barbara said, "Saturday sounds better. We have to meet friends at the country club on Friday evening, and my parents want my sister and me to go along." I agreed that Saturday was much better. We talked the entire lunch period. We walked to the next class that we shared.

After school, I offered to give her a ride home. She said, "I am waiting on my sister." When I politely offered the ride to her and her sister, she agreed. We rode the entire two blocks to her house. Not only was Barbara attractive but she also had the best smelling perfume that I ever smelled in all my life. She told me later that it was imported.

Karl was beside himself when I told him about my date with Barbara. He must have asked a hundred questions. Karl conceded the loss of the race. He was excited about my date and told me that I had better tell him everything about the date.

On Thursday night, my phone rang. I picked it up, thinking that it was Karl wanting to know if I had talked to Barbara. Well, it wasn't Karl. It was Barbara. She told me that she had spoken to her parents about inviting me to the country club on Friday night. They wanted to meet me and thought that it would be a great time to make the introductions. The meeting would most likely be short, as her parents would be busy with their friends.

Barbara and Kate needed someone their own age to talk to at the event. Barbara asked me if Karl would be available to go with her sister Kate. I quickly said that Karl would be more than happy to do so. We went on to discuss Karl's attributes, and I assured her that Karl was above reproach. I went on to say that I had known Karl since we were in the first grade. She agreed that Karl would be a suitable date for her sister Kate.

I went over to Karl's house right after my phone call had ended with Barbara. When I told Karl the arrangements that I had made for him with Kate, he almost fainted. He sat down on the bed, he was silent for a minute or two, and then he smiled. It wasn't as if Karl had any choice; I was insistent that Karl be there for Kate. He agreed to do this for me.

Many years have passed since my first date with Barbara and Karl's first date with Kate. They looked so good together. Barbara and I did too. We were sitting at the best steak place Karl and I could find, celebrating our twenty-fifth wedding anniversary. Karl and Kate were celebrating their anniversary also. Karl and I had dated Barbara and Kate during the rest of high school and all the way through college. Two months after graduating from college, we had a double-ring ceremony, per Barbara's parents' request. We went on our honeymoons at the same resort.

Kate and Karl have two children. They named them Carson and Cameron. Barbara and I also have two children. We named them Kaylee and Kelli. Barbara and I live on two acres. Karl and Kate live on the adjacent property. We are both empty nesters, with one child each in college. Our children are not ready to have children yet, but we are hopeful.

I learned a valuable lesson that day in high school. I thought Barbara was way out of my league and that she would never give me the time of day. What I didn't know was that Barbara had been asking her friends about Karl and me. She had been interested in me for two years, and I hadn't even known it. She was almost ready to make a move on me when fate intervened in that school hallway.

She had wanted me to ask her on a date, but I hadn't known it. The moral of that story is this: There is only one stupid question. That's the one you didn't ask. If you want a date with a girl, ask her. They are only humans just like you are. You never know, but she might say yes, and you may find your soul mate like I did.

There is something to be said about people who meet in life and bond, either as friends or as couples. Karl and I met in first grade and remain friends to this day. Barbara and Kate have always gotten along well together. People used to say that they were not sisters but lifelong friends. We raised our children in good Christian homes.

They did well in school, and although they are cousins, they stand up for one another just like brothers and sisters do.

I know there is a God in heaven. He has watched over us all these years, and he will continue to do so for eternity. God bless you.

The Rewards of Oversleeping

(Based on a True Story)

THE TOWN THAT WE LIVED IN WAS IN THE SUBURBS OF A metropolitan city. It was quiet most of the time. Teenagers always went to the big city to have fun. Our town was known as a bedroom community because most of it was primarily residential. It had the usual businesses, but everyone traveled the few miles to the big city for any major shopping. A lesson was about to be learned by a city employee, which would stay with him for many years.

Like any smaller city, it had its growing pains. The city employed four police officers including the chief, four firefighters including their chief, and various employees in other departments. The firefighters worked a twenty-four-on and forty-eight-off shift. This may seem like a long shift, but not that many calls were received. Sometimes the firefighters get through an entire shift and never answer a single call.

One city employee went on a weekend adventure regularly about every third weekend. He was close friends with one of the firefighters, and every time that firefighter had a shift on the weekend, he would stop by and visit for a while.

Although the city only had only one paid firefighter per shift, this didn't mean that emergencies went unanswered. At that time, the city relied heavily on its volunteer force for support. The city had about twenty volunteers. After the chief went home at four o'clock in the afternoon, the paid firefighter needed a volunteer to assist with a medical emergency. In some cases, the fire chief worked the firefighter's medical call if a volunteer was not available to assist. Sometimes city employees were allowed to assist on the fire or medical responses. Such a city employee visited the local fire station on weekends.

One of the paid firefighters became close friends with this city employee. When the firefighter's shift fell on the weekend, they would visit. Because on-duty firefighters counted on the volunteers, the city employee was at the station if an emergency occurred. The city employee didn't come every weekend, but he was most assuredly there when his firefighter friend was on shift. They became good friends during their tenure with the city and remained friends for many years. The daily routine of the paid firefighter was followed without fail. Each unit, the trucks, and the ambulances must be checked at the beginning of each shift. This was to ensure that each unit was ready for an emergency. This procedure was used by most fire departments, large and small. This city was no different. One of the first parts of the routine was to start each unit and let it run for a few minutes. This ensured that each unit was ready, and the battery also charged while the unit was running.

Another item on the checklist was going to each fire apparatus and changing the water in the water cans. The water cans were necessary when working at a fire scene. It was easy to become overheated at those scenes, so drinking water was valuable. The summers were stressful for firefighters, and water was essential to prevent dehydration. The warning lights and siren were also checked while the units were running.

Another item on the checklist was the two-way radio. The firefighter called the dispatcher to ensure that the unit's radio communications were in good working order. Nothing could be worse than responding to an incident without radio communications.

Other duties were spread throughout the day as well. There was always something to do around the fire station. The building was kept clean, swept, mopped, and organized. Even the bay area was kept spotless. Everything in the building and on the units had its place. This was typical of most fire departments.

The city had four fire trucks. The city also had two ambulances, a boat, and the fire chief's vehicle. There were three bays in the station. The first bay had two fire trucks in it. In the lead was a small engine, which we will call Engine No. 1. It was very effective for quick responses. Behind Engine No. 1, there was a much larger unit, which we will call A-1. This unit was used for grass fires because the water tank held a considerable amount of water. This unit was designated with an *A* because it was not capable of pumping water from a fire hydrant. It was sometimes used as a support unit when not on grass or brush fires. The unit was self-contained. Therefore, it was not an actual fire engine. The unit had dual tandem axles, and it could carry about 1,500 gallons of water. It was a difficult unit to drive and to shift.

The second bay had an ambulance in the lead. This was the primary ambulance used as the first response for all medical calls, major accidents, and large fire scenes. We will call this Medic No. 1. Behind the ambulance was another self-contained fire truck, which we will call A-2. This unit was used for small fires and quick responses. At that time, its primary purpose was to respond to major auto accidents that had injuries. It was standard practice for an ambulance and an A unit to respond simultaneously to all accidents with injuries.

The third bay held an older, large fire engine, which we will call Engine No. 2. This unit would respond to any large structure fire when a supply line had to be laid for a continuous water supply. A second ambulance, which we will call Medic No. 2, was in a smaller side bay. It was only used as a backup when the lead ambulance was unavailable or occupied on another call.

Each fire apparatus, ambulance, boat, and piece of equipment had its place in the station and on each unit. Everything was organized to allow the firefighters to access equipment and tools quickly. Marks were painted on the floor to ensure that each unit was in the correct parking position. Space was critical, as each unit had to be strategically placed for quick responses.

Every fire truck in the fire department was the manual-shift type. These manual-shift units were always backed into position, the gearshift was placed in the neutral position, and the emergency brake was applied to hold the unit in its place. The medic units and the fire chief's vehicle were the only automatic-shift units in the department.

At night when firefighters were awakened to an emergency call, they could be out the door in no more than two minutes. Their firefighter's coats and helmets were always placed in the first-response fire unit. Their firefighters' bunker pants and boots were usually placed at their bedsides for quick dressing. Some firefighters would put their bunker pants in the first lead unit or first out unit.

As I said before, a city employee, who was also a volunteer firefighter, visited the fire station every weekend that his firefighter friend was on duty. Many times, the city employee helped to refresh the water cans or with other tasks. After the daily inspections and checklist were completed, the firefighter and his city-employee friend would sometimes prepare and eat breakfast. The on-duty firefighter was responsible for everything that happened at that station. He was responsible to the chief for the daily checklists. That firefighter would start each unit and perform the radio check himself. No volunteer was permitted to do that unless a paid firefighter wasn't on duty during that weekend shift. In that case, the fire chief would supervise the volunteer during these checks.

One of the city employee's routines was to sit on Engine No. 1's tailboard in the first bay while the firefighter performed his checklist. They would talk in passing while the city employee relaxed on the tailboard. Bay 2's door and the side door were always opened to allow a draft to blow the bay area's exhaust out. The city employee would sit there for a few minutes, reminiscing about the first time he had driven each unit. He would think how it felt behind the wheel of a responding unit as the lights flashed and the siren blared while responding to an emergency call. It was an exciting event for a man in his twenties.

Summertime was busy for all city employees. With his fifth year completed, the city employee was promoted to supervisor. He was working countless hours and helping the fire department in his spare time. The work seemed to be endless. The workload increased in the summer months because of good weather and more daylight hours. The city had every position filled, and there was more than enough work to go around.

That summer was a busy season for grass fires also. This supervisor responded more than his fair share, both in his city job and with the volunteer department. During this period, the state was suffering from a long dry spell, with less and less rainfall that summer.

Everything was as dry as a tinderbox, just waiting for someone to toss out a lit cigarette. It was so dry that a lightning bolt could start a fire by striking the ground. A downed power line in a grassy field could easily start a fire. With dry conditions and wind, a grass fire could get out of control in a very short time.

On occasion, other volunteers would stop by the fire station to visit with the supervisor and the on-duty firefighter. As time allowed, they would sit at the kitchen table and talk about their lives. One particular Saturday, the supervisor brought some food to the station. The firefighter friend had just boiled some eggs, so they sat down at the table to eat. The firefighter saved a few eggs in a bowl to eat later that evening or the next morning. The other volunteer came in and sat down at one end of the table.

As they began talking, the other volunteer took one of the eggs out of the bowl and rolled it in his hand. "Mind if I have one of your eggs?" he said as he cracked the egg on the table. To his surprise, it was raw. He had taken the egg from the uncooked egg bowl and hadn't known it. As that egg spread all over the table, they had a good laugh. From that point on, anytime the volunteer stopped by and saw the two eating boiled eggs, he would ask, "Are these boiled?"

The firefighter would say, "Crack it and find out." He would then place the egg back into the bowl. Things like this would occur at the fire station.

The supervisor spent the following Friday trying to finish his weekly reports and other paperwork. He was always told that the job was not complete until all the paperwork was finished. That was certainly true for city governments. When five o'clock arrived, the supervisor spent the next hour finishing his reports in his quiet office.

He made his routine walk-through of the equipment yard. The supervisor inspected each unit to ensure that the windows were rolled up and doors and toolboxes were secured. His final task was to secure all the gates before leaving for the day.

As the supervisor drove home, a fire call came over the radio. It was a small grass fire. The supervisor responded, along with other volunteers, and assisted the on-duty firefighter in extinguishing the grass fire. The fire took about an hour to extinguish. Based on the burn pattern, it appeared that someone had tossed out a lit cigarette or intentionally started the fire. It didn't matter now. The fire was extinguished.

The supervisor arrived home at seven o'clock that evening. The first order of business was to get out of his smoked-filled clothes and take a bath. He didn't remember much of that evening. He was sure that he had eaten something, watched television, and then gone to bed. The supervisor was a single man, so he spent more and more time at work. He was tired from an exhausting work week, with too many hours under his belt. The night must have been quiet, as the supervisor didn't remember any disturbances. There were indeed no fire alarms that night. He remembered getting to sleep quickly.

The supervisor's friend arrived at the fire station at his usual time to relieve the previous shift. He began the standard checklist of tasks that morning, just as he had done so many times before. It was a typical day in a firefighter's life at this small-town fire station. The firefighter opened the bay door, partially opened the side bay door, and started the units. He always began his day with Bay 1. The large A unit was usually first on his list. Then he moved to the small engine that was in front of it. He then proceeded to Bay 2 and started the lead ambulance and the other A unit behind it. Next, he opened Bay 3 and started the large engine. Last on the list was the backup ambulance. This was always the order for this firefighter's shift. This weekend would start the same way that it always did.

Now the firefighter was a tall man. He was undoubtedly one of the tallest employees that the city had on staff. One volunteer was equal to his height and weight. The firefighter didn't have to climb up into a unit to start it. He opened the door, reached inside, started the engine, and did a radio check. While the unit was running, he then grabbed the water cooler out of the rear compartment and set it on the floor. He then proceeded to the next unit and did the same thing.

That morning, the firefighter opened the large A unit's driver's door, reached inside the unit, and turned the ignition to start the engine. The engine started immediately. But before the firefighter could blink, the large A unit leaped forward as if it were responding to a call but without a driver behind the wheel. The firefighter quickly hopped into the cab and disabled the unit.

The entire event took only four or five seconds. When the large A unit leaped forward, it crashed into the small engine's back. This, of course, pushed the lead engine into the bay door. The front bumper of the large A unit crawled up on the tailboard of the smaller engine. It was a forgone conclusion that extensive damage probably had been done to the bay door. Both fire units were slightly damaged but not beyond use. The damage was minimal to the trucks.

The fire chief was notified of the event. As the chief arrived, he stood there for a minute, gazing at the bay door with the small engine's hood protruding from it. The chief just shook his head and asked the firefighter how it had happened. The chief called a company to come and repair the door and then left. The firefighter backed the units into their starting positions and finished checking the other units.

When he went inside the kitchen, he sat down at the table to relax for a minute or two before writing out his report. As he sat at the table, it suddenly dawned on him that something had been different that morning. The supervisor hadn't show up. He seldom missed his weekend visits, and the firefighter wondered where he was. The supervisor was nowhere to be found. The firefighter spent the next couple of hours thinking about the incident.

Monday morning arrived soon enough. As the supervisor drove past the fire station, he noticed the damaged bay door. He parked and went inside the fire station. The fire chief explained what had happened while they walked into the bay to look at the trucks. The supervisor stared at the small engine's tailboard and then the front bumper of the A unit. A sick feeling came over him as he stood there. He realized that he was supposed to have been sitting on that tailboard on the previous weekend but that he had overslept. The supervisor explained to the fire chief how he usually sat on that tailboard while the firefighter checked the engines. The fire chief shrugged his shoulders and said, "It was a good thing you weren't here."

By the time the firefighter's shift came around again, the door and trucks had been repaired. The supervisor stopped by the fire station on his way home to visit with his firefighter friend. They both walked into the bay and looked again at the two fire units that were parked in Bay 1. As they stared at the tailboard of the small engine, the firefighter remarked, "Thank the Lord you were not here. There was no way you could have moved out of the way in time. The Lord saved your life." The supervisor turned and looked at his firefighter friend and said, "I overslept. When I woke up, it was too late, so I just hung around the house."

The supervisor must have had a guardian angel watching over him that weekend. If he had been there on that fateful day, he would have been killed in that incident. The firefighter estimates that it took about two or three seconds for the A unit to strike the small engine.

Although the supervisor was a young man, he could not have possibly moved out of the way in time. He and the firefighter are both grateful for the Lord's hand in this incident. The supervisor is incredibly grateful for God's mercy that day. You see, the supervisor was not living a Christian life at the time of this incident. I know this story is true. I was the man who missed his weekend visit with his firefighter friend by oversleeping.

This incident was one of many narrow misses by this time in my life. I chose not to see them as a warning. I knew better, but I did it anyway.

The firefighter had been witnessing to the supervisor for several weeks before this incident occurred. Not long after this incident, the supervisor changed his life. He stands grateful to this day.

One never knows where or when one's time is finished on this earth. The warning signs are everywhere if people will open their eyes and look. Your fire-truck incident may not conclude the same way mine did. The Lord gives everyone many opportunities to come to know him. When will your next opportunity come? Will you survive your fire-truck incident? God bless you.

The River

(Based on a True Story)

IT WAS ONLY TEN YEARS OLD WHEN MY DAD DRAGGED ME UP AND down the riverbanks. I was scared to death of the water because I couldn't swim. I heard all my short life that a man from our town had killed a sixteen-foot-long alligator at the river. I couldn't help but think there may be others. I suspect it would be frightening for anyone who chose to wade in the waters of the Nueces River. The water wasn't very deep in most places, but it had tree limbs, and it was narrow at points in the summer; however, it had fish in it.

During March, white bass spawned, and we caught them by the bushel-basket full. We didn't even need bait sometimes. We used artificial lures and dragged in twenty or thirty of them in a matter of a few hours. It was exciting for those who loved to fish like my dad. He fished the river every chance he got but especially in the summer.

Sometimes he went with a couple of his fishing buddies and stayed all night. They ran trout lines and brought home some pretty large catfish.

One time, I remember dad bringing home a huge catfish. He took it to one of the local businesses that had one of those scales on the sidewalk. Our town had a couple of those where you put a penny in the machine and then stood on the platform to weigh yourself. Well, they tried to weigh the fish, but it kept falling off the scale. They had an idea. They put the fish in a cardboard box. They placed it on the scale and put me in the box to hold the fish up. Then they took the fish out and weighed me and the box. The fish weighed more than I did—thirty-five pounds. That was a lot of fish. We took it home, cleaned it, and put it in the freezer to eat later.

Fish was often in our family's diet. It was a cheap source of food for us. All you needed was a cane pole, some fishing line, a hook, a lead weight, and a cork. Most families in my youth had these items and used them often. Bait was never a problem. Depending on the type of fish that we wanted, we had a few artificial lures to use. We also dug up worms to use as bait. We could sometimes use liver for bait. The river was close enough that we could walk there in the summer if we wanted. Besides fishing, my family also hunted.

When I was ten years of age, my dad took me fishing with him one Saturday morning. He had a rod and reel for him and one for me. He had one of those Johnson Century reels that he bought from a catalog, and mine was one that he found while working for the Texas Highway Department. I believe it was a Zebco reel, and it had a six-foot rod with it. It was an excellent rig for a ten-year-old boy. Dad had been teaching me how to cast it, bait it, and set the cork if we were using bait. I had been practicing for about two weeks and anticipating the fishing trip to the river. Now, we didn't have to travel far, as the river was no more than a mile away. We were driving there so carrying everything wasn't going to be a problem.

We left the house as soon as it got light enough to see well and drove straight to the river. We arrived at the boat ramp, parked, and got everything that we needed out of the car. I carried my rod and reel and a can of worms while dad carried everything else. When we got to the riverbank, my eyes grew big, and I began to get nervous. There was a trail on both sides of the river. It was a narrow walking path, but it was also steep and leaning toward the river. You could see that many others had traveled up and down the river using this beaten path. When I got on the walking path, I felt like I would slide off into the river. I was undoubtedly a scared little boy. I even started crying. I was so frightened because I could not swim.

My dad took my hand, and he partially dragged me down the path. We moved three or four times and further away from the ramp. No boats were in the water. We were the only ones on the river that morning for a while.

Dad tested the waters each time that we moved to see if he could get a bite. When we found the spot where he got the first bite, we stopped there. He baited my hook, and I cast it into the water. It didn't take long for that cork to disappear under the water. Dad yelled out, "You've got a bite. Set the hook and reel him in. Pick up your rod and reel in the fish." I did just that. When I jerked the rod, it set the hook just like I had been taught. I saw my dad do the same thing. I thought I had a whale on the other end of the line. It was a small fish and not big enough to keep, as it was under the length requirement. Dad changed my bait, adjusted the cork to a different depth, and I cast my line back into the water.

After a while, I was not as afraid of the walking path as I had been at first. Now don't think my fears completely went away, as they didn't. I was very aware of my surroundings, and my fears were multiplied by the fact that I couldn't swim. That was the most frightening thing, but dad assured me that he could rescue me if I fell in the water. That was comforting but not quite as much as not being there.

We fished for about two hours, and then more people came to the river to do the same. I saw a boy that I went to school with on the walking path. I could tell by the way he walked that he wasn't afraid. I knew he could swim. The next time we moved, I tried not to show any fear, as I knew my classmate was watching me. His dad had drug him up and down those same river banks a while back. He couldn't swim at that time. He told me one day afterward, that he wasn't afraid of the water after he learned to swim. I guess there is a lesson there for me somewhere.

Dad caught four or five fish that we could keep, and I caught one also. I cast out one last time, and down it went. The cork went under before it was even balanced in the water. I jerked the line, and I thought that fish was going to pull me in the water. I called out to my dad to help me, and he held onto me while I tried to reel it in. I couldn't do it. The fish was just too strong for me to handle. I almost lost the rod because the fish was jerking and pulling so hard. I almost lost my grip on it. Dad finally put his hands on the rod beside mine and helped me reel the fish in.

He said, "Let him fight for a few minutes and get tired so you can reel him in. It's a big fish, son. Yeah, you got a big one on the line.

We don't want to lose him for sure." My school classmate was about fifteen feet away and watching the whole thing as it went down. We finally got the fish up to the bank, and dad reached down and picked the fish up by the gills. It was a monster of a fish. I could see that Dad was having trouble pulling him out of the water without falling into the river himself. I called out to my classmate, "Look what I caught. It's a huge fish. Come look at it."

He came over and saw what I had caught and said, "That's a real big fish. Everyone in school is going to be so proud of you when they find out how big this fish is." I knew that he would tell everyone in school about the fish. I wasn't concerned about him telling our friends but about him telling them that I had caught it. I was so proud that I had caught it instead of my dad.

When we were walking back to the car, I asked my dad if we could stop and weigh the fish somewhere. Another couple of guys arrived, and they had a fish scale in their car. We hung the fish on it, and dad held it up. It was a whopping six pounds. I thought that I had a whale there. That was a large fish to be a bass. We didn't have a camera, so we didn't get a photograph of it. I had my classmate's testimony to verify the fish story.

The following Monday morning, my school friend had told everyone in the class, and it spread around the school that day like wildfire. Even the teachers asked me if the story was true. I said, "Yes, ma'am, it's true. You can ask my dad about it if you want." I was the most popular kid in the fifth grade for a day because of my big fish story. I felt like I was ten feet tall, and I was no longer afraid of the riverbanks. When I got into junior high school, my friends and I spent summer days at the river fishing. Sometimes I was glad when we didn't catch anything, as we would have had to carry them all the way home.

Occasionally, we got a ride to the river from one of my friends, who lived two blocks over from me. If it was a Saturday, his dad drove us to the river and came back three hours or so later to pick us up.

When we were catching a lot of fish on those March encounters, we were so grateful for the ride home because we had thirty or forty fish to carry and clean.

I spent the better part of my teenage years fishing at one place or another. When we were of driving age, we went to the lake instead of the river. Of course, we didn't always fish. Sometimes we rode in a boat or picnicked with other classmates and our girlfriends.

Sometimes the youth group at church got together and went to an area lake where someone had a weekend lake house. They were all supervised by the one of the boys' or girls' parents and the lake house's owners. It was fun. Who knew on that frightful day when dad dragged me down the riverbank that it would inspire me to like the water so much?

The Volunteer Reserves

THERE WERE ABOUT SIX PEOPLE IN THE RESERVE POLICE department in those days. They assisted full-time officers and were sometimes unwanted. Comparatively speaking, some of the full-time officers were not exactly top-notch public servants. The reserves were no different. The guys who volunteered for the reserves were just everyday employees who didn't know a lot about police work.

They were asked to help, so they took up the challenge. The reserves and full-time officers did some pretty stupid things along the way. Some people said that they had a makeshift police department.

Perhaps it was only a temporary thing. One could only hope. Football season always brought back memories from our high school days. Many of us graduated from the same high school and then went to work for the city. It was a small city of about ten thousand people, and there wasn't much going on. High-school football games always brought students together to watch our team play. Those were some good times. We had some good times in the police reserves also. Four of us from the old high school days went to work for our small city. The jobs we had didn't pay much, but it was steady work and a living.

Our wives worked, and that made up the difference. Many friends asked why some of us didn't go to college. The answer was simple: We couldn't afford it. The old saying is that the rich man goes to college, and the poor man goes to work. So we went to work. It was not a bad thing. We needed the experience of earning a living to figure out what we wanted to do. I already knew that I wanted to be on the district attorney's staff, but here again, one needed a college education and law school to do that. All of us went to college later in life, and we have successful careers.

Our small town had seven police officers. We had a chief of police, one patrol sergeant, and five patrol officers. If there was any criminal-investigation work to do, it was usually handled by the sheriff's department. Like I said before, there wasn't much going on in our fair city, except on weekends. Most of the time, it was underage drinking, traffic violations, disturbance calls, and on occasion, a burglary or theft. What we now call domestic violence calls were the calls that no one wanted. Who wants to get between a wife and husband when they are arguing and fighting?

Citizens were concerned that our department didn't have enough offices to handle crime in our town. If officers were working a parade or a sporting event, they wondered who was patrolling the streets. It was a legitimate concern. The citizens complained about having more than one officer on duty, but they didn't want to pay the additional taxes to support the cost. I think that is typical even today. The town experienced a bank robbery one time, and it was probably the straw that broke the camel's back. The county handled that investigation.

The city manager decided to form a reserve police department. Most of these officers came from the rank and file of the city's workforce. The reserve force was strictly on a volunteer basis. Although there was no salary, the city paid for the uniforms and other equipment that was used while on duty. The reserves had arrest powers, but they were noncommissioned. To be clear, they were not allowed to carry handguns unless they went to the police academy.

There was a shotgun in the car in case the officer got into serious trouble. As far as anyone could remember, no reserve had ever had to use it. That was another good thing.

The reserves were trained in handguns and shotguns on the gun range by the chief of police. All of us could handle a handgun, shotgun, and rifle. We were all taught by our dads how to use these with safety in mind. We were not afraid to be in the car without a handgun. All of us were too young to be afraid.

One of the primary duties was to ride with commissioned officers, assist with the radio, assist in traffic stops, work the sports' events, and help during parades and other events. Directing traffic at an automobile accident was one of the duties that the reserves performed. The reserves also helped the officers with their reports. I had an excellent printing hand, so one of my functions while riding was to write citations for whoever had the privilege of having me as a partner.

An officer needed someone with him, while he was on duty, to show the public that he was not alone. Perhaps this gave some a sense of not being alone on the streets. I think the citizens had the satisfaction of knowing that there were two officers in the car. It also gave the officer someone to talk with while out on patrol. When working a domestic call, it was nice to have someone with the officer to handle some unruly or intoxicated person. Many times, it was difficult to place someone under arrest when he or she was fighting with the officer. I can recall a couple of those incidents.

Reserves did not ride every shift, especially during the day. Since most were working their regular jobs, some would ride in the evenings until eleven or twelve o'clock. Reserves usually rode with officers on the weekends. If anything was going to happen, it was usually on the weekends or during a full moon. It appeared that crime increased during a full moon. I always thought it was a myth, but I found out the hard way a couple of times.

Riding in a police vehicle didn't make us popular with some of our high school friends or the students who turned to the other side of the law. In fact, we became the enemy to several people whom we had to help arrest for one crime or another. Sometimes I could persuade the officer not to write a citation for one of my friends. I wasn't always successful, but it did happen on occasion. I always felt that a citation didn't prevent a crime; it just encouraged them to do other things. I can remember stopping one of the former high school cheerleaders for driving sixty miles an hour in a forty-five-mile-an-hour zone. She was not happy about the traffic stop and was giving the officer a hard time. I stayed in the car to listen to the radio at first.

When the officer brought her license to check for warrants, he said, "She sure is mad about something. I don't think she likes police officers." I looked at the name on the license and said, "I know her. Do you want me to talk to her and try to calm her down?"

The officer replied, "I think you are barking in the wind, but try it and see how she responds."

When I checked the name and vehicle, she had no warrants or any criminal activity on her record, other than a couple of citations for speeding. I knew before checking her license plate that the car was not stolen. I knew why she only had a couple of citations rather than several. Her father was a prominent person in the community.

Politics always got in the way, especially in a small town. Before I exited the car, I convinced the officer not to issue the citation. He agreed and said, "I wasn't going to write the citation until she got all loud and offensive." Calming the officer and the driver down was something I needed to do for the sake of just getting along with everyone. I knew the longer we detained the driver, the angrier she would get.

The officer did calm down, and I exited the car with her license in hand. I walked up to the driver's side of the vehicle and began to talk to her. She did remember me from high school, and we talked for two or three minutes. I reminded her that driving so fast on the city streets in the dark was dangerous. I also reminded her about an auto-pedestrian accident that had occurred a year earlier where a child had been severely injured because the driver had been going too fast and hadn't stopped in time. Both of us knew the child's parents, and she finally calmed down and realized that we were trying to keep her from having an accident. I handed her the license.

She asked, "You're not going to write me a ticket?"

"No. That will not keep you from speeding. Only you can stop driving so fast so that you will avoid an accident." She smiled, and off she went into the night.

By not writing this person a ticket, we gained a tiny bit of respect—probably a half-teaspoonful. I never worried about people driving too fast when they were not in the residential districts where children played or in a school zone. Other officers didn't care where it was; they wrote the ticket anyway. My objections made me unpopular with one of the officers. I solved that problem by not riding with him. I was not about to risk my life for a fifty-dollar ticket. When chasing someone down, we could risk a tire blowing out. We would be the ones having the accident. That wasn't for me, and that wasn't for the others in the reserves. I think all of us had the same attitude about it.

There are cases when a citation is necessary, but in my opinion, avoiding a simple driving-infraction ticket was a plus. The chief disagreed with us on that point.

Bob was one of our classmates who became a reserve officer. He was a kind and polite man, who would give you the shirt off his back. He was good-natured, and he always had a smile on his face. Not many things could upset Bob. One Friday night, the on-duty officer got sick in the middle of his shift. Bob and I were selected to patrol the city to show that we had commissioned officers on duty. The sheriff's department always backed up the city's officers on serious calls if their officers were in the area. I had just arrived at the police station. Bob was at the gas pumps fueling the vehicle.

While doing so, a bird flew into the open door. Bob didn't realize it right away. The sky began to sprinkle small raindrops, so Bob closed the door. As he swung the door to close it, a stray dog jumped into the car to chase the bird. The bird was flying around the car, trying desperately to avoid the hungry dog. The bird landed on the gearshift's lever, and the dog jumped into the front seat and tried to get the bird. The bird quickly flew out the window with the dog in hot pursuit. Bob closed the window and turned to watch the dog chase the low-flying bird. At that time, Bob noticed that the hose on the gas pump was getting farther and farther away from him. Bob turned around again and opened the door to secure the car. The bird quickly saw the opportunity to return to the vehicle's safety with the dog still in hot pursuit.

Bob stumbled and closed the door, with it still in motion. They were all over that car. The dog stepped on the door lock and then accidentally turned on the warning lights. The bird flew under the seat, trying to hide from the pursuing dog. The dog scrambled to the floor and pressed the accelerator pedal. The car ran over Bob's foot.

The car sped forward as Bob hobbled in hot pursuit of the patrol car. He wasn't about to let that car hit something. Realizing that the doors were all locked, he stopped and watched as the car flew across the parking lot and crashed into the side of the fire station. The loud crash startled the sleeping, on-duty firefighter, who rose to see what had just happened.

The gas pumps were only a block away. When I had heard the siren, I had run that block to see what had happened. I knew that Bob wouldn't turn on the siren unless he was in trouble and needed help. Just as I rounded the corner to the city yard, I heard the car crashing into the building. I wasn't sure at that moment exactly what I was hearing, but it didn't sound good. The siren was still blaring when I approached the car. Bob realized that he had a spare key on his belt. We unlocked the car and turned everything off. The dog was sitting in the back seat with the bird in his mouth. When Bob opened the door, the dog bolted and ran off into the night. The bird was still in its mouth. There went all the evidence Bob had to prove that the dog had wrecked his car instead of him.

The building the car had crashed into was the fire station. The firefighter hurried out the back door to see what the commotion was all about. All three of us stood there looking at that police car and the side of the building. I looked at Bob and asked, "What just happened here, Bob?"

He looked down at his injured foot and said, "No one is going to believe that the dog and the bird were in the car. Who's going to believe me?"

"What dog and what bird?" the firefighter asked. It was fortunate for Bob that I had seen the dog exit the car, but I had not seen a bird. The next morning, the chief of police wanted a report of the injury.

He came over to the area where Bob was doing some light duty in the warehouse and asked about his foot. Then he asked how the incident had occurred. Bob had already prepared a detailed report of the incident. I wasn't there, but I heard the warehouse manager say that later that day the chief said that he had never heard of such a ridiculous thing in all his life. No one could believe what had happened. A bird flew into the car. A stray dog just happened to be there. The dog chased the bird around the squad car and caused it to crash into a building. Whoever heard of such a thing? As I said, I wasn't there, so I couldn't verify the incident, and I was glad. It did sound a little unlikely.

Football games were something that I enjoyed working at. Reserves were deployed at football games to break up fights or arguments that occurred, assist if an arrest was necessary, or help in first-aid matters. We were also there to show a presence in numbers so that people would think the place was swarming with cops. This presence helped prevent activities that caused disturbances. Even though we were there in numbers, there were still incidents that almost got out of control. High school football in Texas was something to behold. People always got into arguments, which were most of the time friendly, when supporting their perspective teams. Texas people supported their local sports' teams, no matter what. Local citizens could criticize the team, but an out-of-towner couldn't. That's just the way it was in Texas.

One night, local football team was playing a rival gang. The game was going well for the locals, but the opposing team wasn't happy. The opposing team accused the referees of cheating. That was not the case, but sometimes people needed an excuse to complain. The score was 21-7, and it was one of those rival games. The local team was winning. I had just come from the home team's side with an officer who had been breaking up what could have been a fight. I was standing next to the ambulance, talking to the firefighter. We were sure that we had a victory.

A radio call came in. "We have a fight. I need help." I ran toward the hometown bleachers. One of the reverses fell in behind me. We were following the sidewalk, trying to get under the bleachers to help break up the fight. I feared that others would join in, and we would have a riot on our hands. Texas football games can get intense at times.

When I got to the bleachers, the sidewalk curved slightly to the right and then it straightened out. The area under the bleachers was dimly lit. The area wasn't as bright as I thought it should be. I zigged right and then left, trying to avoid onlookers. I screamed, "Get out of the way! Get out of the way!" Bob saw a shortcut to avoid the crowd and went left around a group of people. The problem was that the sidewalk went right and then left to avoid one of those round metal poles. All I heard was a loud, "Bong!" The hollow metal pole rang out like a gong. Bob had run right into it. I looked back, and Bob was lying flat on his back.

I could hear his moans and groans over the noise of the laughing crowd of spectators. Bob was stunned and dizzy but not seriously injured. He was going to have a big headache for a few hours. I squatted down and asked, "You OK, Bob?"

"Yes, I think so. Not much hurt but my pride. Is the pole OK?"

The crowd was still laughing, and I quickly yelled out, "Quiet. This man may be seriously injured." The crowd was dispersed to avoid any more embarrassment for Bob. I helped Bob to his feet, and we walked over to the ambulance. The firefighter applied a cold compress on his forehead and gave him an aspirin. We sat there until the game was over without incident.

Bob got over his embarrassment quickly. On occasion, the other reserves reminded Bob about his folly. Bob laughed along with them and went about his business. The pole and Bob were doing well.

Bob hadn't even dented the pole. This incident was a classic case of zagging when he should have been zigging. A good moral to this story is—other than watching where you are going—never take shortcuts. You never know what lies ahead, especially in the dark.

Danger lurks everywhere, even at football games. By the way, Bob has a new nickname. It is Knot Head.

Norman was another reserve that seemed to find trouble and mishaps. Norman was a good guy just like Bob, but he got excited easily. He had a wife and one child. Norman had one problem. Even his wife admitted that he had an issue with this one thing. Norman couldn't put a puzzle together, assemble a bike, hang a picture, or do anything like that. Norman tried many times. His wife didn't let him fix anything around the house. If she couldn't do it, she usually called Bob or me to assist. One day, his wife said that it was a good thing that we were not allowed to carry guns. We knew several commissioned officers whom we thought shouldn't be allowed to carry firearms. Bob and I worked well with our hands, and we could read and follow instructions. Norman was good with numbers. He was our warehouse employee. He could tell you to the inch where everything in the warehouse was located. He knew about bookkeeping also. The city used him to help with the budget. That was Norman's specialty.

One Saturday morning, Norman was riding with our newest police officer. He was only one year out of the academy. He seemed to be a nice guy, but that didn't make a good officer. They pulled a car over on the main drag through town. It was a man in his sixties, and he wasn't giving an inch. Norman could tell that the officer was getting upset. The new officer wrote the man a citation for running a stop sign. The man was not happy at all. He refused to sign the citation.

The officer asked Norman to attest to the man refusing to sign the citation. The older man was handed his copy of the ticket. He immediately tore the citation into several pieces and threw them on the ground. The officer wrote the man another citation for littering. The man tore that citation to pieces also.

The older man told the officer that he had lived in that city all of his life and that there hadn't been a stop sign at that intersection for the last fifty years. The young officer told him that the sign was there. Norman commented that the sign had been installed two weeks ago. The older man agreed to accept the citation and settle the matter in traffic court. When the man left the scene, he accidentally ran over Norman's and the officer's toes. Although he didn't break any bones, they had sore feet for a couple of weeks. Now we had three people with sore feet. What a workman's-comp claim that turned out to be.

Norman and the new officer seemed to get along well together. The new officer requested Norman on the weekends that he was on duty. Three Saturdays later, Norman showed up at three o'clock for his evening shift with the new officer. One of the first calls they received was a nuisance dog call. Ordinarily, police officers didn't work this type of call, but this dog had attacked a man in the street.

As they turned onto the street where the dog was supposed to be, they noticed a man standing on his porch waving his arms. Norman rolled down his window, and the man came out to the car. He told the officers where the dog was. When Norman and the officer went to the next block, there was a small dog that looked like a Chihuahua.

This couldn't possibly be the vicious dog the man had been talking about. Norman and the new officer got out of the car. The dog quickly ran over to the officers, but he wasn't wagging his tail. This was always a bad sign.

The dog barked furiously. The dog grabbed Norman's pant leg, tearing the bottom of his pants. Then the dog ripped a hole in his sock. As Norman struggled to get the little monster off his leg, the new officer came around the car. The dog quickly tore into the officer's pant leg and socks. The dog went back and forth. After a bit, Norman reached down to pick the dog up. That was a mistake. The dog bit his finger. The new officer reached down at the same time, and the dog bit the officer's trigger finger. The dog went back and forth, attacking both officers. They decided to get in the car to avoid the vicious little monster.

When Norman opened his door, the dog jumped into the front seat of the car. When the officer opened the driver's door, the dog snarled and growled at him with all its teeth showing. They were in serious trouble now. The dog wouldn't allow them to get back into the car.

That dog was a vicious little thing. While all of this was going on, people were watching from their front porches. Each of them watched with vigilance. The crowd began to grow, and the dog became more and more vicious. The dog was barking, growling, and snarling. This situation was getting out of hand, and it was no longer a laughing matter. When they tried to capture the dog, it would snap at them and prevent its capture.

They hadn't checked out at their location, so dispatch had no way of knowing what was going on. Norman closed both doors to the car to contain the dog. But when he did, the dog jumped up to the window and locked both doors from the driver's side by stepping on the door lock. Now they had a dilemma. There was a dog in their car, and the engine was still running. The car's doors were now locked, and a vicious dog was inside.

When the dispatcher could not raise the new officer on the radio, she sent a backup. When he arrived, he looked at the situation and laughed. The newly arrived officer walked up to the door, unlocked the door with Norman's spare key, and ordered the dog out of the car. The dog complied. It ran two houses up the street and went through a doggy door into a house. I don't think that I wanted to be the one to write that report. They cleared the scene without an arrest or a citation. It was a good thing that camcorders were not available then. Sometimes one had to know when one was licked, especially by a small dog.

The new officer quit the department on the following Monday.

Norman bought new uniform pants and socks for his next ride along with a partner. By the way, Norman was scared to death of dogs, even before this event. The Chihuahua didn't help matters any.

Dogs would not be Norman's or a seasoned officer's only situation. They encountered a force of another kind two Saturdays later. I couldn't believe what was going on in our department. Everyone seemed to think that the reserves were contributing to an existing problem, and they were right. Guns, dogs, birds, people, and fellow officers would see just how that little department could get into exciting situations.

One Saturday afternoon, Jack, who was another reserve officer, was riding with a police officer. They went on shift at seven in the morning, and they were almost ready to complete their shift. One of the friends he went to school with had asked him to stop by his house. The friend had some kind of situation that he needed to talk to his police-officer friend about.

When they arrived, a neighbor came over to see what was going on. The officer's friend explained that he and some of the neighbors were thinking about buying a handgun and joining the local gun club. As they discussed the thought, the two other neighbors came over to hear the conversation. As they discussed this situation, one of the neighbors asked the police officer what caliber of handgun he carried. The officer replied that he carried a .9 millimeter. The neighbor asked if he could look at it.

It was like nothing Jack had ever seen before. The officer handed his weapon over to the neighbor. Jack noticed a strange smile come over the neighbor's face. The neighbor pointed the gun up into the air and pulled the trigger. Everyone jumped about two feet off the ground. The officer quickly seized the weapon and secured it back into his holster. Everyone laughed, and the officer's face turned pale white and then red. Everyone in the neighborhood heard the gun discharge. Not only was it embarrassing but also illegal to discharge a gun within the city limits.

I found out about the incident that night when Jack called me at home. I wondered who would believe the report, whatever it ended up being. I didn't want any part of that situation, and neither did anyone else.

The officer now had a problem. The offense was a class-C misdemeanor, which was punished by a citation and a fine if convicted. If the officer issued the citation, the neighbor would report the person that he had got the gun from. If the officer reported it, he would be placed on suspension, pending an investigation. At best, the officer would receive some time off if he wasn't relieved of duty.

What could he do? The officer decided to report that he had unholstered his weapon to show it to one of the neighbors. The neighbor grabbed the gun, and it went off accidentally, end of the story. That report may have satisfied the neighbors, but not the chief.

The chief suspended the officer for three days without pay and made it a permanent part of his file.

Jack was the humorous type, and he could think on the spur of the moment. His brain could process information quickly. We thought Jack was a genius, but in reflection, he just had a very good memory. He could tell funny jokes with the best of them and make anyone laugh. He approached one of his coworkers and asked,

"What do you think?" He could start a conversation with just those words. Jack could read a book and remember every event that took place in it. He read the entire *Texas Penal Code* one summer, and he could remember what offenses someone could be arrested for.

Full-time officers loved him for that. Being a police officer was something new for Jack. Every time he turned around, officers were asking him to ride with them. Jack only rode on the weekends. He was a single man in his mid-twenties, and he was a handsome guy too.

The officer that Jack was to ride with that Saturday night was a three-year police veteran. He was what we called gung ho. The chief warned Jack about this officer and instructed him to help keep him on track. Jack agreed that he probably needed medication to slow him down a bit. The officer moved quickly everywhere he went. He did have one good quality. His uniform was always clean, pressed, and neat. His shoes were always shined to a military standard. He had the personality of a turnip. Now, if there was a fight to break up, he could handle it. If an officer needed help with an unruly suspect, he was the one to have around. Of all things, his nickname was Turnip. Most thought the green end of the turnip was the reason for it.

That Saturday night, all was going well for the two patrol cars on the streets. One car had two reserves in it, and the other had a full-time officer and a reserve. Jack was the reserve riding with the full-time officer. The two reserves were assigned to patrol the local shopping center and watch for people parking in the handicapped spaces who were not handicapped. This must have been a real problem for the businesses and the department. I was in the reserve car, and it was a boring night. The other assignment that we had was to watch the teenagers' hangout for any sign of trouble. The only problem that we saw was the teenagers throwing water balloons at passing cars. They quickly dispersed when we arrived.

The full-time officer and Jack had just received a call from dispatch. It was a silent alarm at the only sporting goods store in our city. With lights blacked out, they pulled in behind the store in the alley. There no cars parked in the alley, but there was a broken door.

The reserves parked in front out of sight of the burglars. We did our part and parked. We could not have apprehended armed suspects. We were there to let the armed officer know which way they went if they escaped.

Jack stayed in the car by the radio. The full-time officer went inside with his flashlight and gun in his hands. The officer left his flashlight off to avoid detection. When he was about in the middle of the store, he came around a cabinet where the men's clothes were. All of a sudden, he saw a figure staring right at him. The officer quickly raised his gun and fired one round. He thought that the bullet would surely hit the target center mass. He was wrong. The image fell into a thousand pieces. The officer had shot his reflection in a large upright mirror.

When Jack heard the gunshot, he radioed in for assistance. The reserve car quickly drove to the back of the store. The dispatcher called a county deputy. He happened to have a car stopped on the highway, about three blocks away. When the officer inside the store saw what he had done, he was embarrassed but certain that the burglars were inside the store. The officer kept searching for the burglars. Jack was afraid to enter the store, fearing he would be mistaken for the officer. This was probably the only smart thing that they did at the scene. The deputy arrived within minutes. The deputy entered the building with his flashlight turned on. He called out for the city officer. There was no answer. The deputy called out again and entered further into the store.

He found the city officer lying on the floor. He used his handheld radio and called for an ambulance.

The deputy called for the reserve officer to come inside. It took both of them to carry the officer out of the building. The deputy ordered the other reserve car to the front of the store, just in case the burglars tried to escape. The ambulance arrived in a few minutes.

The officer was unharmed. The deputy and the reserve went inside and searched the building. There was no one in the store. The deputy scratched his head and said, "If there is no one here, who did the deputy shoot at?" The answer would be something for the books.

The dispatcher had already called the owner of the sporting goods' store. When he arrived, he turned on all the lights in the store. Upon investigation, the city officer saw a reflection on a poster of a hunter dressed in camouflage and supporting a rifle. This accounted for the shot, but what happened to the officer? The deputy and Jack couldn't find anything wrong with the officer. The ambulance crew couldn't find anything either. But they were able to determine what had happened. When the city officer saw the reflection in the mirror, he fainted. His gun went off when he hit the floor, shattering the mirror. The owner stood there looking at the damage. His comment was one for the books. "I am glad I didn't have a fire."

As it turned out, the burglars had been long gone when the officers had arrived. After a careful store inventory, there was only one item missing: the mirror that the officer shot. The only damage was the back door. The burglars must have seen the patrol car speeding across the parking lot with no lights on. They jumped the fence in the ally and got away.

One of our new officers was called to a disturbance in front of a downtown business. Bob was riding with him. When they arrived, they found two men struggling on the sidewalk. The officers quickly separated the two men. One accused the other of trying to take his wallet away from him. Bob took one of the men and placed him in the back seat of the car. The new officer talked to the other man, and he was convinced this man was the victim. He had the appropriate identification in his wallet. He was released from the scene.

After returning to the police station to interrogate the suspect, another reserve walked into the station. He greeted the suspect, called him by name, and asked why he was there. The new officer told him that he was under arrest for trying to steal another man's wallet. The new officer stopped dead in his tracks and asked, "What did you say his name was?" The reserve told him. The officer turned red in the face. He realized that he had the victim in custody and that he had let the thief go, with the victim's wallet. The wallet contained $600 in cash. All this time, Bob had been trying to figure out why they had taken this man into custody.

Bob put him the back seat so that he could separate the two men until they could get the whole story. The man's wallet was found in a trash container a block down the street. It contained everything except the cash. The perpetrator was never found. The man sued the city, and he was awarded $600 in cash as a settlement and an apology. Bob got a letter of commendation for finding the wallet. The officer received a letter from the chief too. It was not a commendation.

The city officers had issues also. Many times, they were no different from the reserves that rode with them. One day, one of the full-time officers had checked out for lunch at a local restaurant. Bob and Jack were going to the same restaurant for lunch. The officer parallel parked his car. Jack and Bob parked in the lot across the street. The place would soon be crowded, so everyone was in a hurry. Bob and Jack looked both ways before crossing the street and waited on a fast-moving pickup. The officer saw them waiting to cross the street. He wanted to get into the restaurant before they did.

When he slung the car door open, he heard, "Bang!" The police car's door went sailing down the street. The pickup that Bob and Jack were waiting for had hit the door at thirty miles an hour. The door broke off at the hinges, and it went sliding down the pavement in front of Bob and Jack. They watched as the door slid and landed up against a no parking sign.

What a way to spend the lunch hour, Bob and Jack thought as they finished their lunch and tea. The officer spent his lunch hour completing an accident report with the patrol sergeant. I don't think the officer enjoyed his lunch break as much as Bob and Jack did.

They were asked to come to the station after their lunch to give their version of the accident. I don't believe Bob and Jack ever rode with that officer again. At least, the officer never requested them as a ride-along partner. Things like this seemed to happen in our small town. I don't know if it was bad luck or the people that the city could afford to hire.

Perhaps it was for the best. The city had adequate insurance, and most of the employees were hometown folks. In a small town, nothing goes unnoticed. By the time the sun came up the next morning, everyone in the city knew the story. I wondered, though, how far out of proportion the story would get after three or four callers told it. I am telling it exactly as it happened. Everyone else can draw their conclusions.

The reserve police program was eventually discontinued, not because of Bob and the pole but because of a safety issue. The sheriff's department argued that the reserve officers should carry a firearm for their protection. The city manager refused and disbanded the program. The city manager went on to bigger and better things. Since Bob had a college education, the city council offered him the city manager's position in our fair city. While Bob was city manager, he attended police academy and became a commissioned police officer.

Because the city could only afford four full-time police officers on the payroll, it sent five other city employees to the police academy. After graduation, they became the new reserve police department and assisted the four full-time officers with their duties. If a police officer became ill, newly armed reserves would assume his shift. Other mishaps occurred during the reserve officers' shifts. Most of them, we cannot discuss, as they were settled out of court for undisclosed amounts.

The following year after implementing the new noncommissioned reserve police department, the city's liability insurance doubled, and repairs to the four new police cars that the city had purchased did as well. Some of the vehicles even had to be replaced. After three years, the mayor and city council decided it was less expensive to hire experienced police officers. The council voted to suspend the reserve program, much to Bob's dismay. After a reserve accidentally shot his dog when it jumped into Bob's brother's squad car while on a traffic stop on the mayor's street, the mayor was the tie-breaking vote. Bob's brother, Wilfred, said that he had just seen something get in his car while writing a ticket for a young female who was speeding through the neighborhood. The traffic citation that Wilfred issued was later dismissed.

Bob opened his own insurance company, which caters to small cities. He tried unsuccessfully to get the legislature to pass a malpractice insurance program for police officers. Bob also owns a salvage yard for wrecked police vehicles. His brother, Wilfred, is the business manager. Jack, Norman, and I kept our city jobs for a while after that. All four of us went on to attend and graduate from college. Norman went on to work for a larger city and took early retirement. He is working on a second career at the sporting goods' store. As for Jack, he went on to become a firefighter in a larger city. He will retire this year as deputy chief. All four of us remained friends through our careers.

I guess I am the last. I went on to graduate from the University of Texas School of Law. I went into private practice after five years with the district attorney's office. One of my moneymakers is defending cities in liability suits. For legal reasons, I cannot discuss their cases.

You can be assured that I have plenty of cases in my files. If the original four officers would have continued working for the city, I would be a millionaire by now.

The Woman in 5B

(Based on a True Story)

APARTMENT LIFE WAS NOT WHAT TOM WOULD HAVE CHOSEN for himself. He had accepted a position in another city, moved most of his belongings to storage, and rented an apartment. Instead of buying a house right of way, he thought he would let the dust settle before making that decision. Tom decided to live in an apartment complex for the first six months. He figured it would take that long for things to balance out with his job. Tom needed to concentrate on the job before buying a house. The job was in his chosen profession, and he knew that he could do that job well.

Tom hadn't been sure about the housing market in the new city. With two large manufacturing plants in town, the housing market might be difficult. One of the guys at work suggested that he wait until a large company laid off workers or others were transferred. Then he could get a good deal on a house. That sounded reasonable, so he waited.

It had taken a little longer than he had expected, but all was well with his job. Things were beginning to shape up, and he even got a promotion when his boss left for another job. Tom was happy about that. Tom watched the news every evening to see what was going on around town. In the meantime, he was making friends in the apartment complex. Tom and his neighbors even cooked out together. All was well except for the holidays. Christmas came and went without much activity. He had no one to celebrate with, so he went out to eat at a local restaurant. The food was good, but there were no leftovers. One must take the good with the bad. At least he had a good meal.

Tom joined a local church and soon made friends with other members. Things were picking up now. He eventually started going to lunch with other church members, and life was good. Tom was a charitable person, and his finances were in good order. Tom had sold his house in his previous city, and he didn't owe anyone a dime. He had no debts and earned a good salary. Tom gave regularly to his church and helped others when he saw the need. He could afford to do so, and he made good use of his finances.

Tom had a heart for the elderly, especially those who had a hard time paying bills and buying things that they needed. He was always doing things for those senior citizens who couldn't do for themselves. Sometimes, he went to nursing homes and visited with people. So many times people in those places didn't have visitors. Tom called them the forgotten ones, whom people put in homes and forgot.

Tom carried on conversations with the people he met. They were such knowledgeable people, and they had lived through some of the most difficult times in our history. Some were even veterans who had stories of their own to tell. Tom was certainly interested in hearing their stories. Sometimes he would read the Bible to those with limited vision. They appreciated his company, and Tom was glad to do it for them. When Tom would miss a visitation, the people missed him and told him so. Tom was so glad that others appreciated his efforts. It wasn't a burden for Tom. He loved visiting with people and hearing about their journeys in life.

One Saturday afternoon, he noticed an older woman walking to her apartment. She was long past her prime, and Tom said something to her as they passed. The woman spoke in return. The two of them would often be at the mailbox at the same time. They stood there and talked for a few minutes, just visiting about daily life.

She told Tom that she had divorced many years ago. She used to clean apartments for extra money, but she was now unable to do that. She was drawing from Social Security. Tom could tell that she was struggling to pay the bills. She didn't let on that she didn't have much money, but Tom could tell by the way she answered questions that she was struggling financially. Because of Tom's heart for the elderly, he was sympathetic and understanding. Tom had struggled financially in his early years. Those were difficult times for several people.

About a month later, Tom saw the woman pulling a cart with wet clothes in them. As they passed each other, she mentioned that her washing machine had gone out. She would wash her clothes in the complex's laundry and then dry them in her apartment. After a month of doing that, Tom felt sorry for the woman and wanted to help. Tom wanted to help, but he didn't yet know how. Tom knew the elderly woman was not physically able to keep this up, especially during the winter. This would create a different dilemma for the woman. The outside temperatures in the winter were sometimes brutal. Tom knew he had to do something.

Tom mentioned this dilemma to one of his fellow church members. As they discussed the matter, the associate pastor said they would help with laundry expenses if needed. Tom wasn't so much concerned with that, as he could do that. As they talked further, the member happened to remember that Sears had washer-and-dryer sets on sale. The member knew that because he had just replaced his set a week earlier. The member suggested that Tom anonymously purchase a washer-and-dryer set and have it delivered.

Tom went to Sears the next afternoon and looked at its inventory. Tom had been in the woman's apartment before. He knew that her washer was green and her dryer was white. Tom could easily afford any set he that he chose, but he wanted to get the right one for her apartment. Tom decided to select a white washer and dryer. This color would go with anything, but the important factor was that they would be new and that they would have a warranty. They would work for a long time without difficulty. Tom's helpful nature was about to benefit someone once again. He made the purchase.

The Sears' salesperson was instructed to have the set installed and to haul off the old washer and dryer. She was also advised not to reveal who had purchased the new washer and dryer. She said the delivery and installers would have no way of knowing who had purchased the machines. Tom could help the woman in apartment 5B without her knowing who had done this wonderful thing for her.

Tom was excited to do this for the elderly woman. Perhaps seeing how God helps those in need would persuade the woman to go to church. Well, it was the thought that was in Tom's mind. Tom wanted God to get the credit and not him.

About a week later, Tom was at the mailbox. The woman in apartment 5B happened to be there getting her mail also. When Tom walked up to his box, the woman greeted Tom and said she had had a surprise happen to her the other day. Tom inquired as to the nature of the surprise. She gladly stated that someone had purchased a new washer and dryer for her. The guys from Sears even installed them and hauled off the old ones. She appeared to be happy about the gift.

Tom replied with innocent eyes, "Well, that's great. You see, God does listen to prayers. How do you like them?"

The woman replied with some dismay in her voice, "It was a good thing to get a new washer and dryer. But I wish they would have asked me first. They are the wrong color. I wanted the washer and dryer to match my refrigerator. I asked the man if he could exchange them for the right color, and he said no. Isn't that just awful. I don't understand why the men wouldn't go back and get the right color washer and dryer."

Tom just stood there in utter disappointment. He couldn't believe what he was hearing. Tom could only think of one thing to say. He looked at the woman and said, "Well, guess we shouldn't look a gift horse in the mouth." The woman chuckled and walked away. Tom stood there for a few minutes. He couldn't believe what he had heard. Tom had a difficult time understanding the woman's attitude.

The following Sunday morning, Tom told the story to his friend at church. They both chuckled for a moment. Tom's friend said, "Some people are like that. They want the blessing but on their terms. You did your part, Tom. You gave that gift in good faith. Don't let her rob you of that blessing."

Tom smiled and said, "No, I saw a need, and I fulfilled that need. I didn't want the woman to know who the gift came from. I didn't want any credit for the good deed. You just can't please everyone. I know God deserves the credit. He put me there and gave me the resources to make that blessing happen. Praise be to the Lord."

Not everyone who receives a gift will appreciate the blessing.

Some people will never understand how God works. The woman had a need, and it was fulfilled. God provided Tom as the means to resolve the woman's dilemma. So many people fail to see the forest for the trees. I guess the moral of this story is not to rob someone of their blessing. When a people give, they receive a gift in return. That gift may not be material things. If a person gives from the heart, God sees and knows that. God bless you.

The Man on the Bus

RIDING THE LOCAL TRANSIT SYSTEM HAS ITS BENEFITS AND downfalls. Most people think that the best thing is having an inexpensive way of traveling around their community without the expense of automobiles, insurance, fuel, and maintenance. The bus systems were put in place to provide transportation for all the citizens. Most larger cities have this type of system. A person can meet some interesting individuals on local buses.

Most of the passengers ride the bus because they have no other means of transportation. It is a different world all together. The downfall of these systems is that they don't travel to all parts of the city. Waiting at a bus stop can be intimidating or frightening to some.

The weather plays a part in the waiting also. The rain, wind, freezing weather, and hot sun can be a deterrent.

People from all walks of life have at one time been on a bus. Those who have no need for public transportation will not commonly be seen as they drive themselves to their destinations. A few years in the past, some of these people were once in a better place in society. Many are still in the dilemma of having to choose between a meal and a bus ticket. Perhaps they must choose between paying the rent or for a child's Christmas present. No matter the dilemma, these people are survivors, the persistence of existence, and the results of our social criteria.

Society knew a man like this. Everyone called him Charlie. He looked old, but in reality, he was sixty-seven years of age. Time and occupation had taken a toll on his body. His tanned skin indicated that he had spent a great deal of time in the sun. His rough-looking hands were of someone who worked with his hands. He wore an old hat that could stand a good brushing or perhaps a replacement.

Modern medicine and good health care allows some people to live into their eighties, into their nineties, and even to the age of one hundred. No, Charlie was not old by years but by life's experiences.

Many wondered where Charlie came from and sometimes questioned where he was going. Most thought Charlie rode the bus so that he could have people around to talk to, although he didn't talk much. Charlie smiled, sat there in his favorite seat, and read his Bible most of the time. Occasionally people asked him what he was reading. He answered by giving the book and chapter. Almost everyone knew Charlie by name and usually greeted him with, "Hey, Charlie," as he took his seat in the middle of the bus.

Now Charlie carried his Bible around in a small zippered bag. The bag had been given to him for Christmas a few years earlier by one of the bus riders. In Charlie's bag was his Bible, a bottle of water, a small snack, a notebook, an ink pen, and a pencil. An old photograph was tucked away in one of the side pockets. The photograph was of a young woman and a little boy of about ten years of age. The notebook in his bag contained notes that he took each time he found something in the Bible that he wanted to remember. The notebook was almost full, and very soon, he would have to replace it.

Charlie lived in a small two-bedroom house in the lower-income part of the city. He did have an old 1950s model pickup in his garage and drove it to the grocery store and to church. Charlie rarely drove it other places. He chose to ride the bus most of the time. His neighbors said that he was a quiet man but that he often helped his elderly neighbors with small projects around their houses. He was well-liked in his neighborhood, but no one really knew him. Charlie's yard was always in good condition and the property was well-maintained.

Some commented that he had had a wife and two children some years ago. Others said that his wife and child had left him twenty years earlier when he got sick. They say he spent two months in the hospital recovering from his illness. No one could remember why.

One day, one person on the bus said that Charlie's wife hadn't wanted to have a sick husband, so she and the child had moved to another city in the East. No one knew for sure if these stories were true or false.

Charlie studied his Bible for hours each day. Anyone who looked at his tattered book could see that it was worn. The pages were all there, but the edges of his Bible were frayed. Charlie knew this famous book better than most people did. Some say he must have been a preacher somewhere or perhaps went to seminary to have such a vast knowledge of the Bible's contents. Anytime anyone wanted to know where a scripture was, he could tell them and even explain it.

Charlie was often the brunt of jokes while riding the bus. Some people would make fun of him while he read his Bible. He was called all kinds of names: Preacher Man, a bible thumper, and a tired old man. He was called more vulgar names by those who were offended by his knowledge of the Bible. Many of the younger people made fun of him because of his clothes and shoes. Charlie wore faded blue jeans, a work shirt, a worn-out belt and work boots. Although they were clean, they were tattered also, just like his Bible.

During the winter, he wore a Viet Nam era jacket, which he had purchased from Goodwill. The fact is that most people thought the rest of his clothes came from Goodwill or were donated to him. He had the look of a poor man who lacked the proper funds to purchase nicer clothes.

Charlie always carried a few coins in his pocket and a senior-discounted bus ticket in his wallet. His other pockets contained a handkerchief and some keys. His shirt pocket contained his reading glasses. One could say that Charlie traveled light. He once said of himself, "I don't have need of much, so I don't carry much." Anyone who knew Charlie would say that he was a simple man who loved the Lord. He had more faith in the Lord than any ten people in his community.

One April afternoon, a young man from one of the Christian schools boarded the bus. That young man asked Charlie about a particular verse in the Bible that he was studying in his school.

Charlie said to the young man, "Son, you have to use the twenty-twenty rule. You can't take one word or one verse and build a ship. You must know what that scripture is talking about." The young man learned so much in his thirty minutes on that bus. He would consult with Charlies many times over the next couple of months about the meaning of scriptures in the Bible.

It was August in Western Texas when the young man got on the bus. Anyone who looked at him could tell he was trouble. Charlie was seated in his usual seat in the middle section of the bus. The young man entered the bus, paid his fare, and then told Charlie to move out of his way. Charlie pulled in his feet so that the man could pass by. The young man made another demand. "Not your feet old man, move out of my seat." Charlie got up and moved to another seat on the bus. Two stops later, Charlie exited the bus to pick up a couple of things from the grocery store.

When Charlie returned to the bus, the young man was gone so he took the same seat that he had when he left. Only three people were on the bus. Several seats were vacant. Two of these people got off at the following stop. Now it was just Charlie and one elderly woman.

At the next stop, the rude young man got back on the bus. As he paid his fare, he turned to Charlie and demanded his seat. Charlie just sat there, unimpressed by the young man's demands. The young man then demanded the elderly woman's seat. Charlie spoke up to say, there are plenty of seats, so take one. The elderly woman asked the young man to take a seat so the bus could leave.

The young man hurled a couple of insults at the elderly woman and Charlie, but they just sat there. Charlie looked around and said, "There are plenty of vacant seats on this bus. Please choose one for yourself." Charlie was still sitting there when the young man grabbed the elderly woman's purse and began taking money out it. The woman screamed and demanded her purse and money back. The young man laughed and cursed at the woman.

Charlie stood up and politely asked the young man to return the woman's purse along with her money. Charlie looked deep into the young man's eyes and just stared at him like a statue. The young man blinked and then dropped the purse, the money, and Charlie's bag on the floor. He backed away toward the back of the bus as if he was afraid of something. Charlie picked up the woman's purse and money. As he handed it to the woman, he said, "There is nothing to fear. He will not bother you again." As all sat down, the bus began to move again.

When the bus reached its midpoint on the route, it stopped to allow passengers to change busses. The elderly woman rose from her seat and said, "Thank you, and may God bless you."

Charlie replied, "It wasn't me. It was the Lord who spoke to the young man."

The woman had a puzzled look on her face as she exited the bus. The driver, now outside the bus, told the elderly woman, "I've seen him do that before. He is God's servant."

Charlie remained on the bus, just sitting there humbly and silently.

The young man darted from the bus. Anyone could tell that he had been affected by something. The look on his face said it all. It was as if he had seen a ghost. His face was pale, and he was trembling.

When Charlie had faced the young man, he hadn't uttered a word. Perhaps there had been a communication that only Charlie and the young man had heard. Perhaps God had spoken through Charlie. The driver believed that Charlie knew what had happened, but he wasn't saying anything.

The following Monday, the young man boarded the bus again. Charlie wasn't there. The man was angry about something, but no one knew what it was. As the young man sat down, the same elderly woman looked him in the eyes. The young man yelled out at the woman, "What are you looking at?"

The elderly woman turned, smiled, and said, "Someday, young man, you will understand what happened the other day. I just hope it isn't too late." The young man looked at her, but he didn't say a word. The elderly woman could see that something was troubling the young man.

A mother and her two children entered the bus and sat down. With all passengers aboard, the bus began its outbound route. About ten minutes into the route, one of the children began gasping for air. She began to shake and fell to the floor. The woman called out to the driver to stop the bus. As the driver pulled to the curb, she opened the door and called 911 for an ambulance. The mother didn't know what was happening. "She's not breathing. She's not breathing!" the woman shouted. The little girl turned different colors as she lay there on the floor. "Please, someone help my baby girl! I don't know what to do." The child had stopped breathing, and her mother cried out for anyone to help her child.

They could hear the siren in the distance. The little girl lay there lifeless in her mother's arms as the girl's mother held her child tightly and sobbed. Then two figures appeared beside her. One figure looked a lot like Charlie, except he was younger. The other was clothed in white with a covering on his head. The Charlie figure took the child from the mother and laid her down on the bus seat. The man clothed in white laid his hand on the other man's shoulder. The man who looked like Charlie looked up toward heaven and laid his hands on the child. The smell of incense filled the bus. Then a cloud of fog surrounded the outside of the bus. The inside of the bus became bright, and a haze filled it. The passengers were afraid, and some began to weep while others began praying for the child. A voice that sounded like thunder calmly said, "Have no fear. The child will recover."

With one hand on the child and the other raised toward heaven, the man bowed his head in prayer. A silence fell over the bus. Even the sounds from outside could not be heard. In a moment, the child began to breath. She awakened, smiled, and looked into the man's eyes. The little girl said, "I've seen you before. You came to me in a dream. Don't be afraid of him, Mother. He knows Jesus." With tears of joy, the child's mother gasped, grabbed her child, wrapped her arms tightly around her, and began to weep in thanks. Everyone closed their eyes and thanked God for the child's life.

When the mother of the child looked up, both men were nowhere to be found. She exclaimed, "Where did they go?"

"I don't know. I looked up, and they were gone. They just vanished," the driver said in disbelief. Everyone on the bus had seen the men, but no one could attest to their whereabouts. They had been there, but then they were not.

The paramedics entered the bus and tended to the little girl. All the child's vital signs were perfect. "What seems to be the problem? We can't find anything wrong with this child," the paramedic asked.

The mother, tearfully, said, "I believe she is going to be fine now." The paramedic suggested that she be checked out at the hospital. The paramedic commented, "You know, it took us a while to find the bus. When we were in route, fog drifted in, and we could not see ten feet in front of us. Then the fog lifted, and the bus was right in front of us. Something strange was going on out here."

The woman looked up and said, "That wasn't strange. A miracle happened here today."

The paramedic laughingly said, "It was a miracle we found you guys in that fog." Everyone on that bus knew what had happened, and it wasn't something made by a human.

Three days later, one of the passengers who frequently rode the bus entered it. The man began to talk to the driver while the driver waited for the other buses to arrive. The man asked the driver, "Did you hear about Charlie?"

"Yes, I saw him put his hands on that little girl, and she came back to life."

"What are you talking about? When did that happen?"

The driver answered, "Monday afternoon. Didn't you hear about that?"

"That's impossible," the man answered.

"No, it really happened. I saw it happen right here on this bus," the driver exclaimed.

The man replied, "That sure wasn't Charlie who did that. He died this past Sunday. He was found still kneeling by his bed on Sunday morning by one of his neighbors."

The driver stood there in disbelief. She was talking to herself. "How can this be? I saw Charlie and another man right here on this bus. I saw him lay his hands on that girl. I saw the miracle God did through Charlie. How can this be?"

The passenger said, "Are you sure it wasn't last week sometime."

"No," the driver replied. "It happened on Monday afternoon just like I said."

The passenger replied again, "Well, something is sure strange here. I know Charlie died this past Sunday. I live right down the street from him."

The driver sat there in disbelief. She knew for certain what she and others had seen on the bus. The driver asked once again, "You say Charlie died. How did he die?"

The passenger said that Charlie had been at the convenience store just a block from his house. A man at the store was asking Charlie if he played the lottery. Charlie politely told the man that he did not gamble. He went on to explain that the Bible said that we shouldn't do it. The man was laughing at Charlie, cursed, and then put a lottery ticket in Charlie's pocket. The man went on to say, "You look like you could use a few dollars, old man. Here is a winning ticket for you." The laughing man exited the building saying, "If that old man wins, I'm going to get my ticket back." The passenger told of how two men were waiting down the street when Charlie got home from church on Sunday night. The passenger said, "Charlie must have been praying just before he went to bed. The police think it was robbery. The house was left in a mess. They found Charlie's Bible on the seat of his pickup.

The passenger went on with his story by saying that the police had located his daughter and former wife. The daughter was thirty years old now. Charlie's daughter was contacted again by the attorney, who said that she was mentioned in his will. When the daughter arrived, she didn't remember her father but claimed his estate. Charlie's estate amounted to over $27 million. The lottery ticket won a total of $10 million after taxes. Charlie had his assets placed into a trust. The lottery ticket was claimed by Charlie's trust."

The story ended with a statement from Charlie's lawyer, who had conveyed the story to Charlie's daughter. Charlie suffered after he served the Vietnam War. After returning to the states, he fell ill from the effects of Agent Orange. But God healed Charlie from his illness.

Charlie used the GI Bill to start a business, and that business was financially successful. Charlie made a fortune in his days after his wife left him. It appeared as if everything that he touched turned to gold.

Charlie came to know Christ when he was forty years old. He made a promise to God that he would only spend enough money to live on if God would take care of his daughter. Charlie lived up to his promise. From that day on, Charlie spent most of his time helping others. Charlie's daughter visited her father's grave after the finances were settled. Charlie's daughter had a beautiful granite marker placed on his grave. An inscription at the bottom read, "To a true servant of God. Until we meet again." You see, Charlie's daughter found out the truth from the attorney, who happened to be Charlie's brother. Charlie's fortune was in good hands all those years, waiting for the daughter to return. The trust Charlie set up paid every penny of his daughter's education, without her knowing of the money's origin. Charlie's daughter set up a trust for the miracle child's (the child whom Charlie had helped save) education in the amount of $150,000.

Shortly after Charlie's death, two men were arrested for Charlie's murder. The district attorney's office filed capital murder charges against the two men. In that indictment, a clause was entered that no death penalty could be brought against the two men. They went on trial the following year, and they were found guilty. They each received life in prison without the possibility of parole. Three months after they had entered prison, Charlie's attorney had sent a package to the two men. The package contained a Bible, a copy of Charlie's Bible notes, and Charlie's life story. It was unknown if the two men repented, as they refused visits from the attorney. The attorney was asked why he had sent the packages to the prisoners. His answer was simple, "We wanted to provide them with all the information they needed to come to know Christ. They have the rest of their lives to decide."

Everyone should know that God moves in mysterious ways and uses odd instruments and strange methods. He works miracles through people as he did on that Monday afternoon. There were witnesses to what happened on that bus. No one could deny that a miracle had occurred. The child and her mother could certainly attest to what had happened that Monday. There were other things that happened that day. The child's mother found work, and her husband did too. Although she has an automobile now, she still rides the bus.

The woman shares her miracle with others. As for the young man who was so rude and vulgar, he later went to seminary. He preaches the gospel in a small church not far from where Charlie lived. As for the miracle child, she is an honor student. She shares her story whenever she can.

God does use people to do his work, but those people must be willing to surrender their lives to what God had in store for them. Each individual has a choice. If a person takes the first step, God will take all the steps with that person for the rest of his or her life. That individual must willingly believe in Christ, just like Charlie does. Yes, I said does. You see, Charlie is not dead. He is walking with the Lord in heaven, just like he did when they walked onto the bus that day.

God bless you.

ABOUT THE AUTHOR

Roy E. Staggs grew up in a small South Texas farm and ranch community. Oil and Gas were discovered on many of the farms and ranches in and near the community and life changed for many, except for his family. He was raised by an alcoholic father and a mother who tolerated the effects of domestic violence in the family. At the age of fourteen, his family moved from the small-town life to the suburbs to Dallas for a life change, where he graduated from high school.

Ray would leave home at his earliest opportunity and go on to have two families of his own, two sons and a daughter. Suffering from the effects of growing up in this situation, he later discovered that his father was suffering from PTSD after serving in a combat role. His father chose alcohol instead of counseling, but Roy would choose to put his life together upon finding the Lord. He fell away from church after episodes of family failures but returned to faith after a twenty-five-year absence.

Roy would go on to put himself through two years of college while working fifty-and-sixty-hour weeks. The difficulties of this would cause him to burn out after only one semester at the University of Texas. Life would deal him his share of difficulties and near-misses, but all would be overcome by his faith in the Lord.

Late in life he married a Christian woman who has been an inspiration to him and maintain a Christian lifestyle. She has had a major influence on Roy and is his best supporter and critic in writing this book.

Roy went on to have a forty-year career in municipal government serving in public utilities and other services in government. After retirement, his thoughts were to write a book. After years of writing policies, procedures and reports, he decided to write a crime mystery novel. When it was almost completed, he found a man who flew with his father during World War Two and this inspired him to write this book.

Roy continues to write and do research and plans to offer the fictional crime mystery and other books sometime in the near future.

www.ingramcontent.com/pod-product-compliance
Lightning Source LLC
Chambersburg PA
CBHW021617120626
46545CB00001B/279